MEN
LOVING
THEMSELVES

images of male self-sexuality

photographs and text

Jack Morin

concept and editing

Joani Blank

book design

Jack Morin
Don Propstra

ISBN 0-9602324-5-1

Library of Congress Catalog Card #80-52942

Down There Press
P.O. Box 2086
Burlingame, California 94010

INTRODUCTION

The men who volunteered to be photographed for this book have relatively little in common; they are about as heterogeneous as any group of twelve adult American males can be. They range in age from the early twenties to the late fifties. They represent a broad spectrum of racial groups and cultural backgrounds. Education and income levels, political and religious beliefs, body types and, of course, personalities all vary considerably. Some are involved in monogomous sexual relationships; some have multiple partners; and some have only casual encounters. Each has his own favorite sexual activities, and no two have the same preferences. Some are straight, some gay, some bisexual. Although each now feels comfortable with his sexuality, most have had to overcome the negative effects of misinformation and early messages about sex.

One of the few things these men do have in common is a positive attitude toward self-pleasuring and masturbation. However, the frequency with which each masturbates varies markedly. The place of masturbation in their overall sexual behavior patterns is also highly variable. Yet, each values this aspect of his sexuality. In this respect, they are different than many men who devalue masturbation, compare it negatively to sex with partners, feel guilty about it and are thus reluctant to explore its full potential.

Another important characteristic shared by all of the men is their willingness to be photographed while masturbating and to have these photographs seen by strangers. Each man's decision to be photographed was motivated primarily by a hope that doing so would be useful to others. They felt this way in spite of their awareness that some people would inevitably have negative reactions to what they were doing and, consequently, to them. Clearly, each had considerable self-confidence, and perhaps a flare for adventure. There were no doubt other internal rewards for some of them (for example, a feeling of self-affirmation, the excitement of being appreciated by unknown viewers, or the fascination of seeing themselves from an external point of view). None of them is or ever has been a professional model, nor will they receive any money for participating in this project.

A large number of men were invited to participate. Most were unwilling to be photographed. Some refused because of negative attitudes toward masturbation. Some felt good about masturbation, but refused out of fear of possible consequences (being ridiculed by friends or colleagues, losing a job or upsetting a lover or family member). Others were too embarrassed or anxious about "going public" with such an intensely personal aspect of themselves. More than twenty-five interested men discussed the idea further in one or more interviews.

The photographs were taken during one session of several hours, in a setting chosen by each individual. My role as photographer was—as unobtrusively as possible—to capture on film each person's usual ways of pleasing himself. I avoided giving directions. The sessions usually included frequent breaks and relaxation periods to neutralize self-consciousness and performance pressures. Each participant feels that the resulting photographs are an accurate reflection, both in content and tone, of his typical masturbation experience.

At another time, each man made a personal statement, either in writing or in a taped interview. The statements, which appear with the photographs of each person, express some of their feelings toward self-sexuality and how it relates to their overall sexual expression. The men were asked to leave the gender of their sexual partners ambiguous (except in a few instances where this could not be done without distorting what they were trying to say). Sexual orientation is relevant to self-sexuality only insofar as it influences fantasy. Nonetheless, knowledge of the subjects' sexual orientations might lead to stereotyping and limit the ability of some people to identify with the photographs.

The statements and photographs give us a rare opportunity to observe an aspect of male sexuality which, for most people, has been shielded from view and largely absent from conversation (except jokes). It is, therefore, not unusual for people initially to feel uneasy as they look at the photographs. Although we have become desensitized by a steady barrage of photographic images, they still can be somewhat stunning in their capacity to reveal—even more so when the subject matter is emotionally charged. As photographer, I, too, have felt moments of embarrasment while working with such personal material. Noticing one's own reactions, whether positive or negative, can be instructive and beneficial.

There are several perspectives from which the photographs can be viewed: simply as an enjoyable visual experience; as a means of exploring, and perhaps questioning, attitudes toward masturbation; as a catalyst for discovering, rediscovering or enhancing actual experiences; or as a starting point for intimate discussions with a friend or lover.

The final section of the book, entitled "The Psychology of Male Self-Sexuality," provides a conceptual framework for understanding the uses of masturbation. The complex psychosocial dynamics which often inhibit self-pleasure are also explored. Practical suggestions for enhancing self-sexuality are included as well. Many men (women too) have found these useful in adding subtlety and depth to the sensual and sexual experiences they have with and for themselves.

MARVIN

Masturbation has always been a highly pleasurable activity for me. As an adolescent I remember being in ecstacy as I rubbed my penis coital fashion against the bedsheets. As I grew older and became involved in sexual relationships, I masturbated less but still enjoyed it a lot.

At one point during my marriage I felt guilty about masturbating. I felt I was cheating on my wife since I usually fantasized during masturbation about another woman with whom I had had a very intense sexual relationship.

If I am feeling tense, depressed, or just plain lousy, masturbating brightens my mood a great deal. Sometimes during graduate school I find myself paralyzed with anxiety about beginning to write a paper. If I take time to masturbate (even a "quickie") I unblock the paralysis and free up energy to write.

When I am feeling really good about myself, I can get very turned on by seeing an attractive woman on the street. I become very horny and begin to fantasize about that person. I can hardly wait to get home so I can continue the fantasy while masturbating. Some of my most deliciously satisfying orgasms happen this way.

I love being outdoors—hiking, backpacking, canoeing, lying naked in the sun. Just recently I have begun to masturbate outdoors as well. Some of my most intense orgasms have happened while the gentle wind caresses my body and the golden sunshine warms me.

When I am in a hurry and trying to force an erection and a climax sometimes I lose sensation and I do not enjoy the experience much. But when I am taking my time, focusing on the pleasurable sensations, and trying different strokes on different parts of my body, then I have very intense orgasms, sometimes even without erection and/or ejaculation.

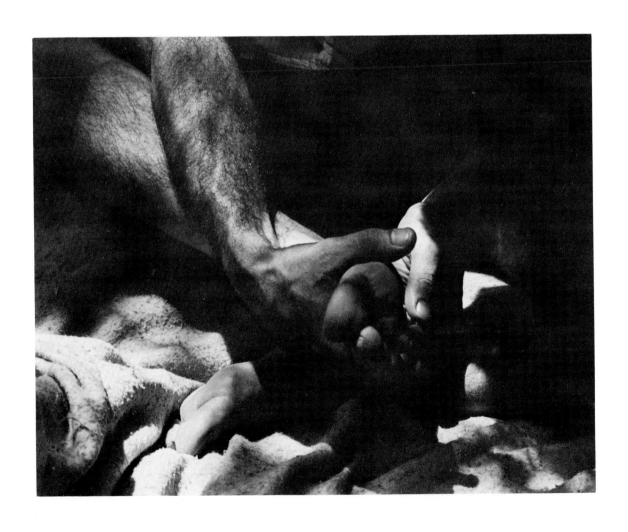

BILLY

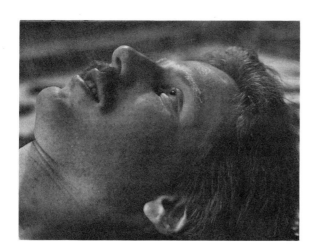

I first experienced pleasure touching my body when I was 12 years old. I was recuperating from surgery and had been flat on my back for six weeks when I discovered that my body had changed radically. I had grown three inches, lost 20 pounds and had sprouted little hairs on my chest. I found that it felt wonderful to stroke the front of my body and my genitals. Within a few weeks I started ejaculating and I have been enjoying masturbation ever since.

My father never talked to me about sex. My mother was very open and tried to talk about sex with me, but I was resistant to discussing it with her. I never felt guilty about masturbation but I knew it was a very private activity. To this day I find that I am more into masturbation when I am living alone and have more time to myself.

As a teenager I used a lot of magazine pictures to trigger my masturbation fantasies. Now my imagination works much better. Most of the people in my fantasies are acquaintances who are not available to me as sexual partners. In those fantasies I am always in control, the dominant partner, while in real life I like to be passive or submissive some of the time.

My favorite times to masturbate are when I wake up or in the afternoon. It seems to give me energy. I also find that it relieves tension when I am feeling uptight. Occasionally, I will do it secretively in some public place where the slight risk of getting caught adds to the excitement. Unlike a lot of men, I do not masturbate when I am horny and am without a partner.

I think masturbation is healthy, exciting and fun. I am real open to exploring new ways of enjoying it myself and want to share it more with partners as well.

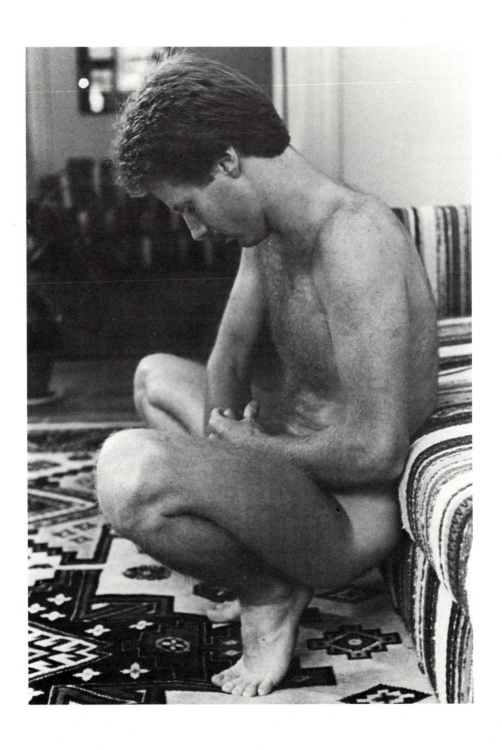

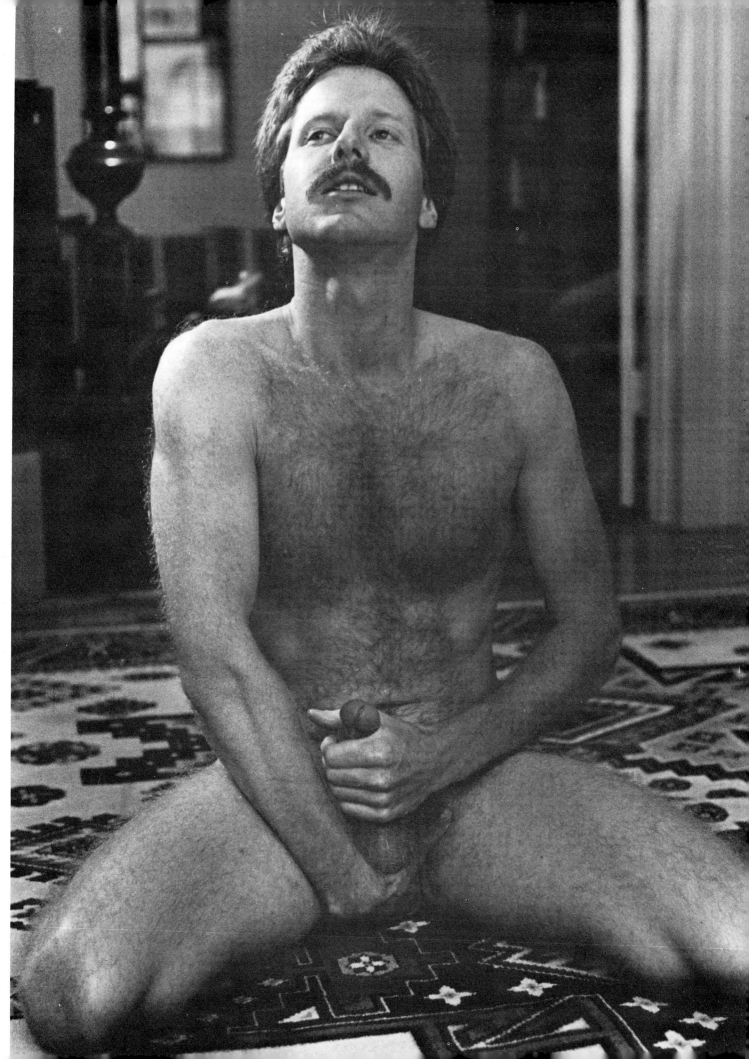

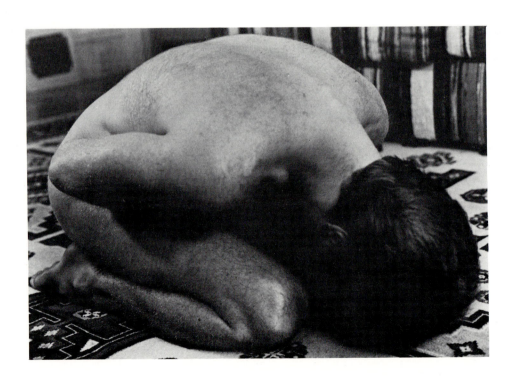

RUSTY

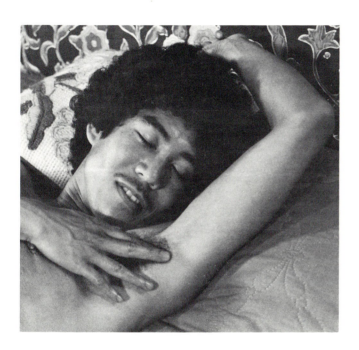

As a kid I was warned that masturbation was bad and that terrible things would happen to me if I did it. I had learned to masturbate by myself and this didn't stop me. I kept it a secret, of course. I thought I was the only one doing it until it dawned on me that there wouldn't be so many prohibitions unless others were doing the same thing. Even though later I heard guys joking about masturbation, I still felt guilty.

It wasn't until I found out I could masturbate with partners that I started to feel much better about it. Now it is so natural to me, it's hard to remember what all the fuss was about.

Sometimes—like after working all day—I want an orgasm as quickly as possible to relieve tension and help me unwind. Other times I masturbate for pleasure. Then I take my time—sometimes an hour or two. I like to embrace myself. My entire body is involved. I like to build to orgasm slowly.

For me masturbation is quite different than having sex with a partner. When I'm with a partner, my attention is focused on that person. When I masturbate, I focus on myself—including my fantasies. I like to fantasize about past encounters I've enjoyed. It's like an "instant replay" that I can run whenever I want.

I'm always discovering new things about my body—new areas to focus on which I'd pretty much ignored before. If I didn't

masturbate, I doubt that I would know
nearly as much about what feels good
to me.

When I masturbate to relieve tension,
after I come it's all over. When I do it for
pleasure, orgasm is not the end. I continue
enjoying myself. Occasionally, I'll have
a second orgasm, but it's not as intense as
the first. After my first orgasm, the whole
experience seems more down to earth.
It's slower, less urgent.

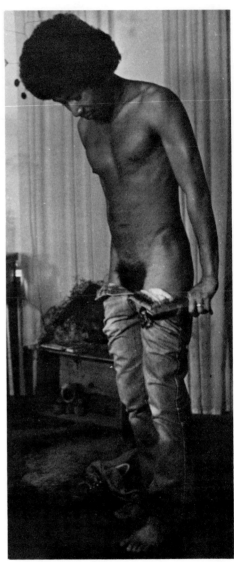

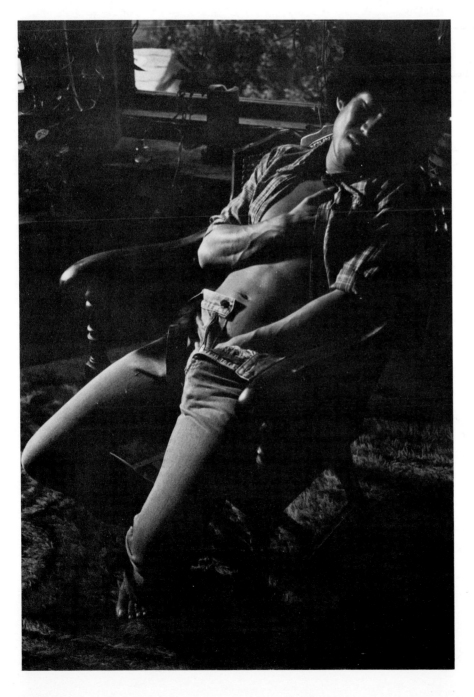

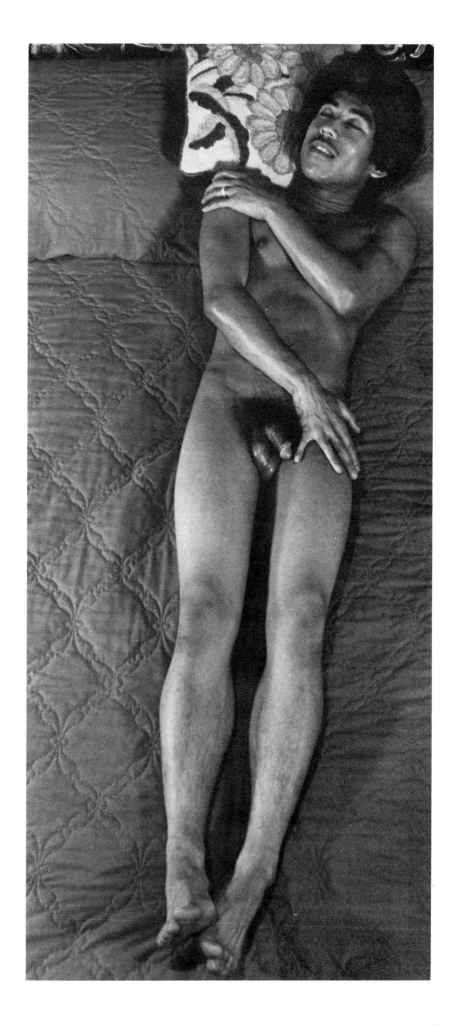

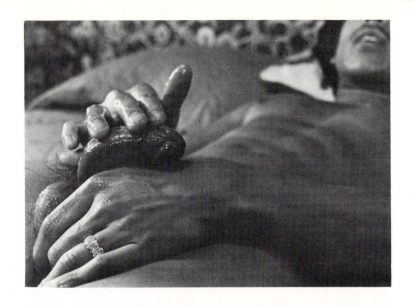

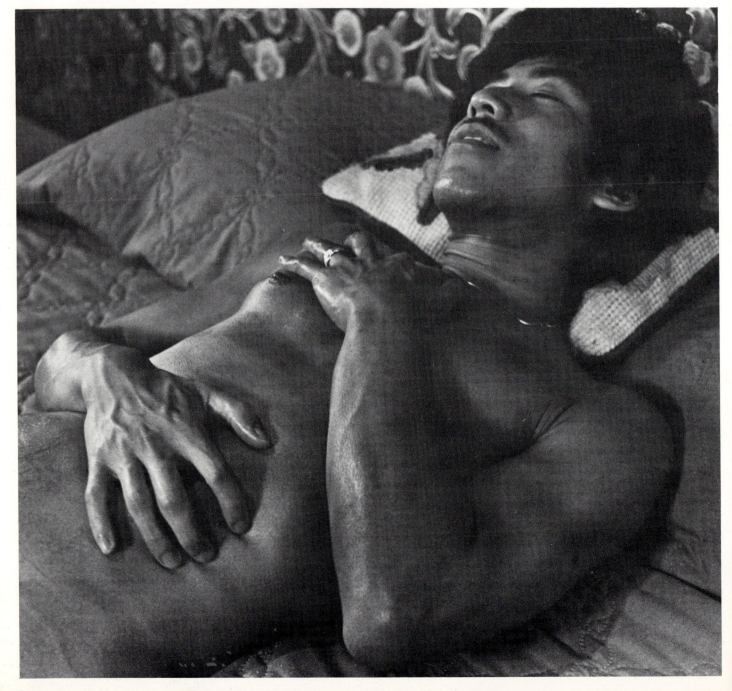

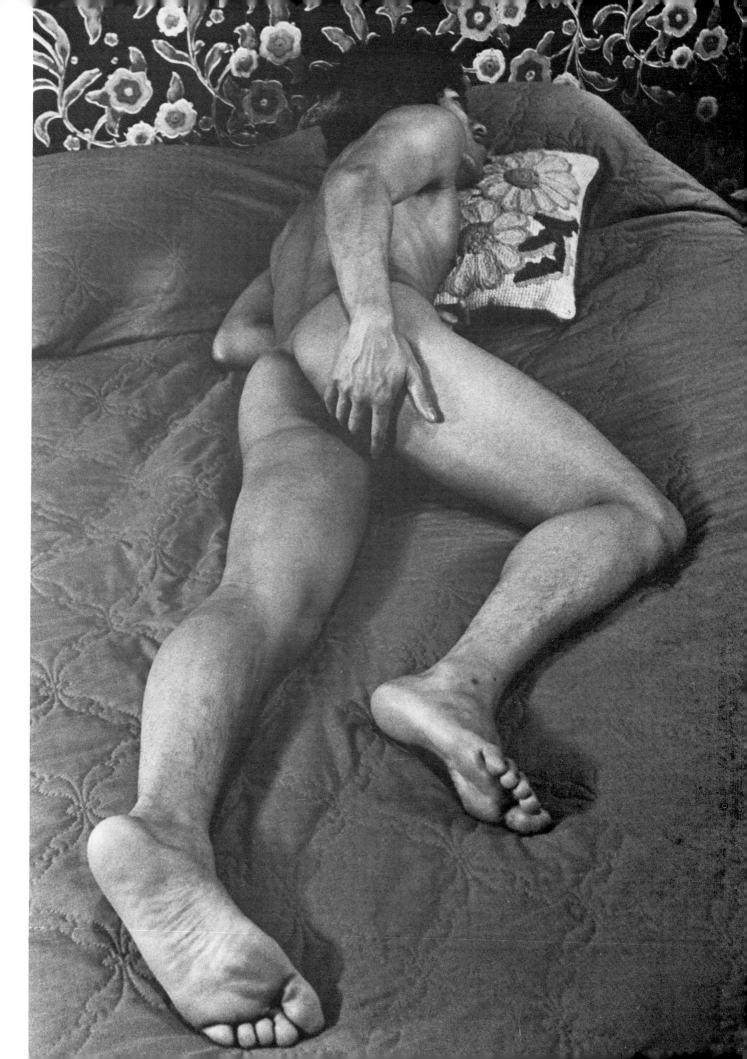

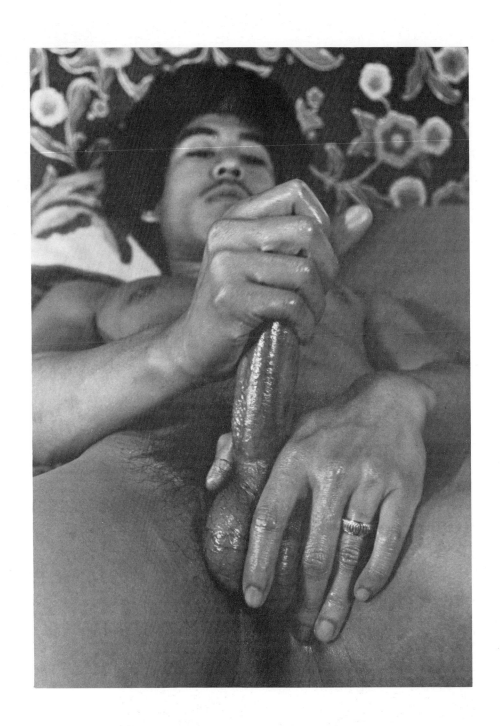

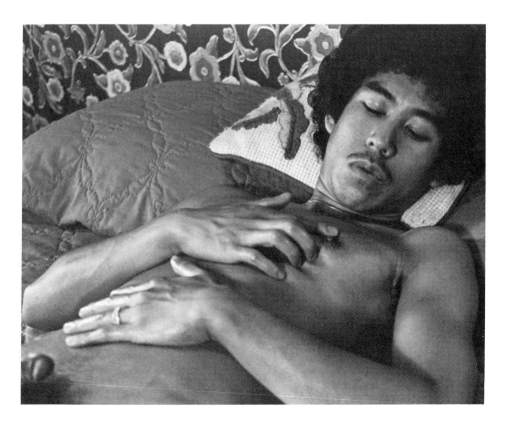

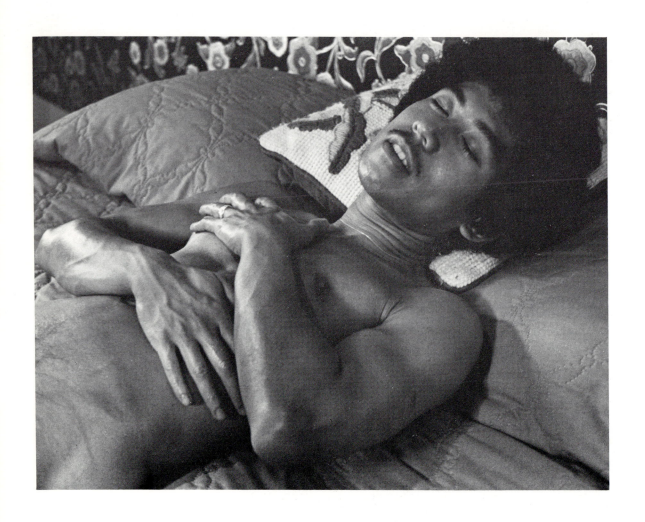

DON

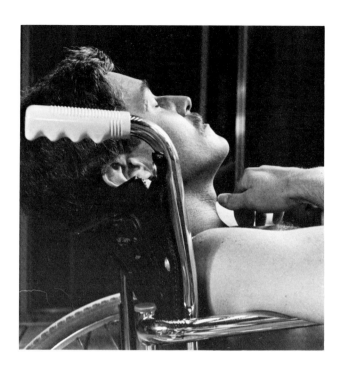

My first sexual experiences were self-loving, only back then we called it self-abuse. Whatever you call it, it felt good to me. My penis was the be-all and end-all of my pleasure. My total attention was focused on it and on "getting my rocks off."

Then at age 19 I injured my back surfing. My body was suddenly very different. I had no sensations below my chest—including my cock. So I figured sex was over for me. I stopped masturbating and stopped thinking of myself as a sexual person.

Luckily my desire to be sexual did not stop. As I experimented with my new body, I learned new ways of pleasuring myself. I listened very carefully to my touch, focusing my attention on it as if it were a whisper. The touch then seemed louder, and as the volume increased I became excited.

New areas of my body became erogenous. My wrists, arms, armpits, chest, nipples and neck became more sensitive and were sources of pleasure. Slow light stroking now coaxes up goose bumps that are followed by grins!

Feeling the fleshy warmth of my cock in my hand is and always has been enjoyable to me. The feelings I get from my penis are subtle. I feel them mostly in my abdominal area. When I am aroused my stomach muscles tighten, my nipples get hard, a sex flush spreads over my chest and goose bumps cover my body. I find it a real visual turn-on to watch the goose bumps rise. Sensations intensify and are at their peak after I ejaculate.

Masturbation for me is an awakening. Loving my whole body has made me aware that my "penile perspective" was limiting and that almost any area of my body can bring me pleasure.

I love touch—anywhere, anytime!

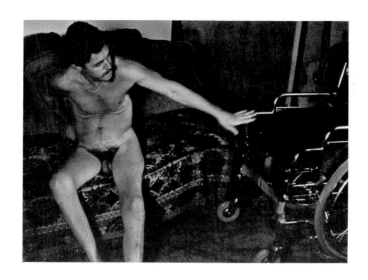

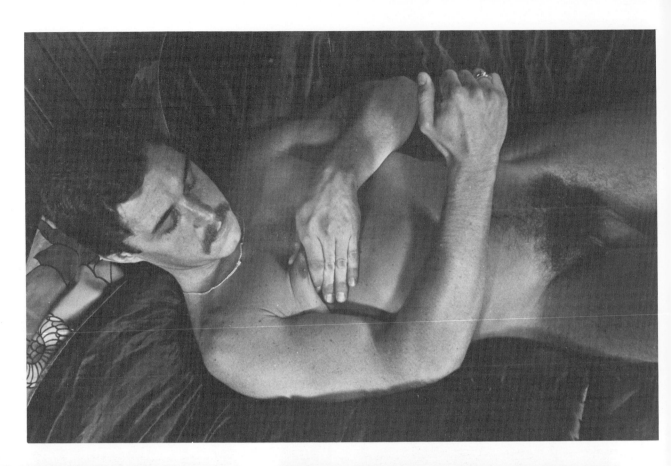

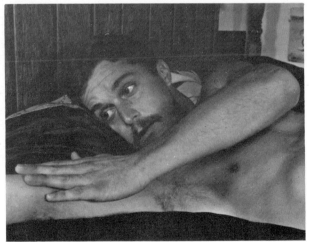

JOHN

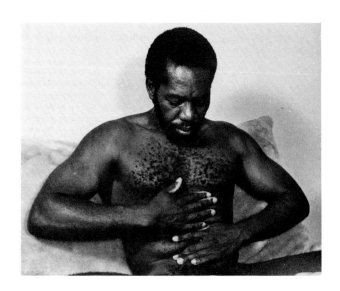

I grew up being aware of a taboo concerning "playing with myself." I learned from my elders that it would "cause you to go crazy, stunt your growth, and cause 'it' to fall off." Guilt and physical threats were the order of the day. The good feelings that I got from playing with myself were stronger than the fear of punishment, however, so I continued. But I did it secretly and hurriedly. It was a frenzy of huffing and puffing, straining for sexual release, always expecting someone to catch me. Afterward, I was sure that everyone who saw me on the street could tell what I had just been doing. I smelled of guilt! I was ashamed and dirty, vowing I would never do it again. How soon the body forgets.

Those frantic five or ten minutes have developed into hours of joy and pleasure that is not goal-oriented, but is a slow process of exploring my whole body— seeing, knowing and understanding. I look upon my body and it is good. I pleasure my body and that is good. I no longer hear the footsteps of Guilt.

I usually begin my sessions with a set of stretching exercises to loosen up and prime my body. I want it to be ready for love— yes, I love myself. I slow my breathing to match my movements. I apply oil to my body. I like the feeling of a finger on my foot, knee, inner thigh, balls, cock, nipples and lips—a slow caress wherever it feels good. I listen to my body's responses. On those occasions when a partner is present and can share masturbation, spoken words lend another's permission to my self-pleasure. Rarely will there be a quick climax, often no climax at all. A few sessions have lasted off and on for an entire night. My mind and body never develop that high level of tension that demands release, but I remain highly aroused, drifting back and forth between a semi-dream sleep and a throbbing, horny awakening.

Masturbation does not reduce my desire for involvement with a partner. It often intensifies it. When masturbation is part of what I do with a partner, I feel that we are sharing something very personal and this can bring an extra feeling of closeness.

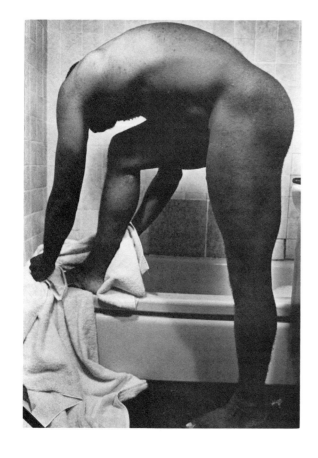

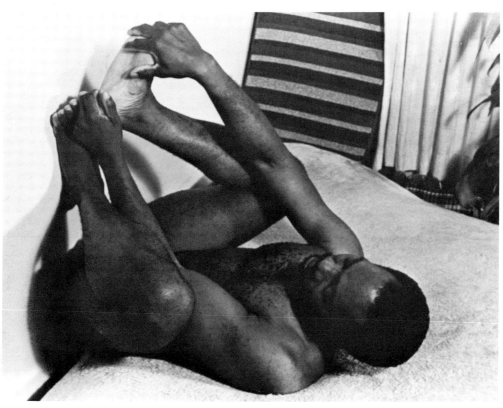

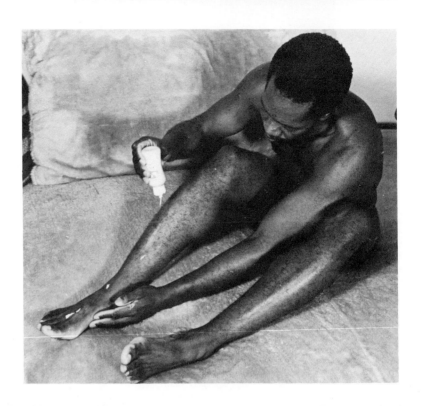

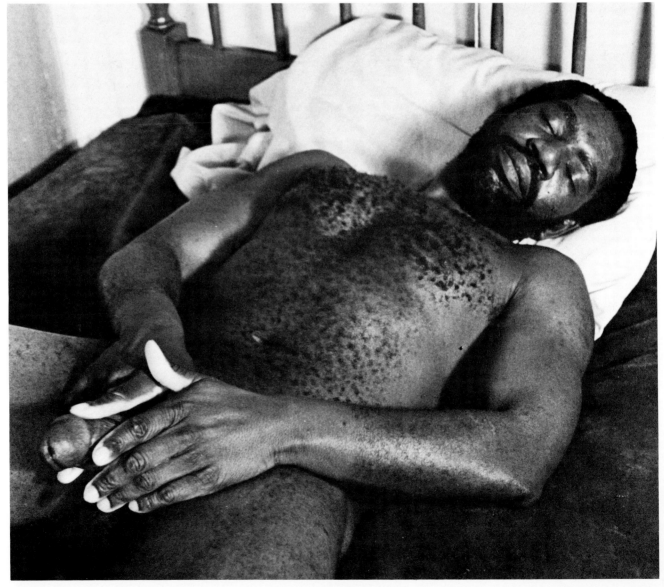

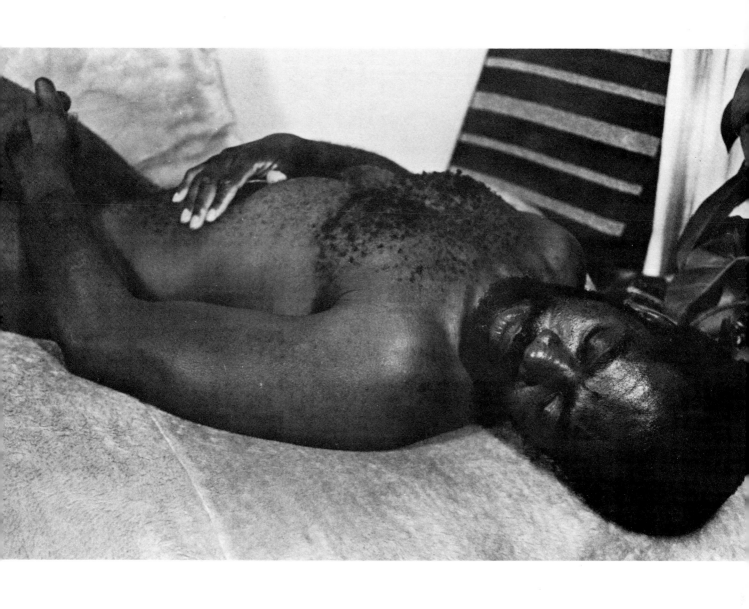

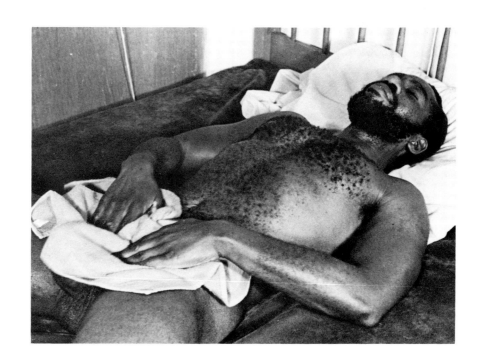

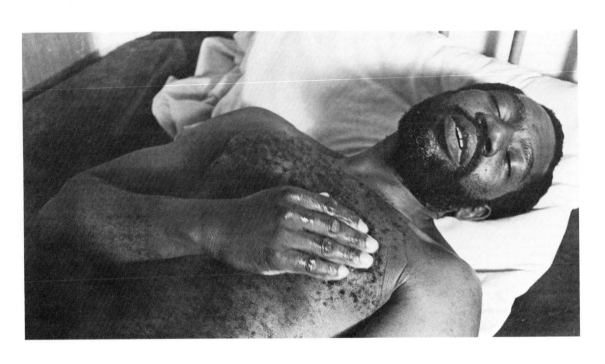

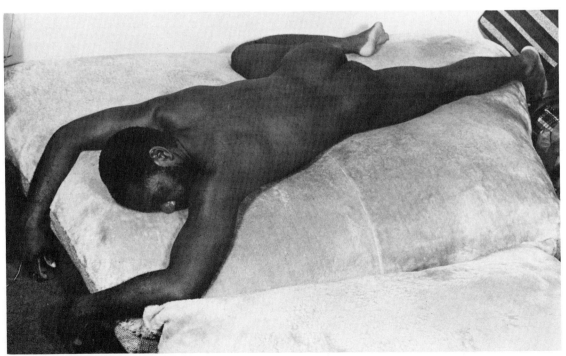

TED

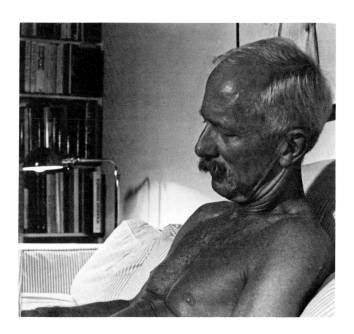

I discovered masturbation accidently when I was nearly thirteen. A friend and I were up in a tree, of all places. It was a very hot afternoon and somehow we had our cocks out and were playing with each other. I'll never forget that first orgasm— watching the semen fall to the ground from the branches of the peach tree. It was totally unexpected. But it was wonderfully pleasant and has ever since remained so.

From the beginning, I have accepted masturbation simply as an exciting thing to do and, luckily, I have never suffered any qualms or guilt about it. As I grew older, especially when I joined the Army, I became far more sexually active. I engaged in all kinds of sexual activities. But by the time I was about 30, I realized that jacking off was pretty central to my fulfillment. Getting to know people who felt the same—which wasn't at all difficult— helped me realize that my preference was really quite acceptable.

The joy that I get from masturbating alone is never very far from me. As time has passed, though, I've found the masturbation experiences I share with a partner to be the most pleasing and satisfying. I feel maximum pleasure when all of the following are involved simultaneously: visual enjoyment of each other, a strong tactile connection between us, and self-touching. If I'm emotionally close to my partner, the affectionate aspects of sex become very important to me. And when I find somebody sensitive enough to jack me off with the same sort of touch that I use with myself, it's truly exhilarating.

If I'm really soaring, masturbation becomes almost mystical or metaphysical. You could say it's a spiritual thing. For me, this is basic and transcends all the other things I can say about jacking off. This can happen with or without a partner. But if a partner feels the same sense of going beyond the usual confines of consciousness, then we can gradually prime each other for a rapturous explosion.

Sometimes this is most powerful when movement is kept to a minimum, allowing awareness of more subtle sensations to build. The words are difficult, but at its most intense, there is a feeling of being united with the cosmos, that fundamental whatever-it-is which keeps us all going. The wonderful thing is that I can do this for myself almost any time.

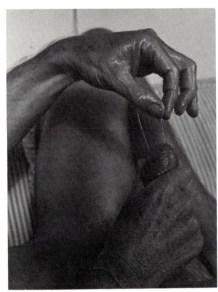

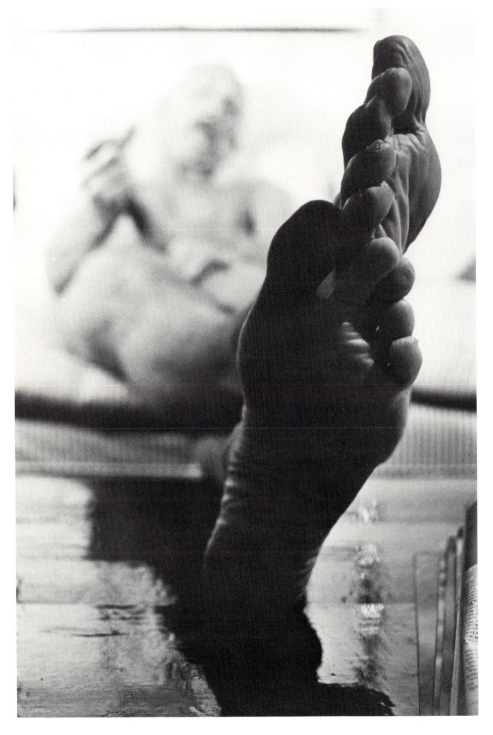

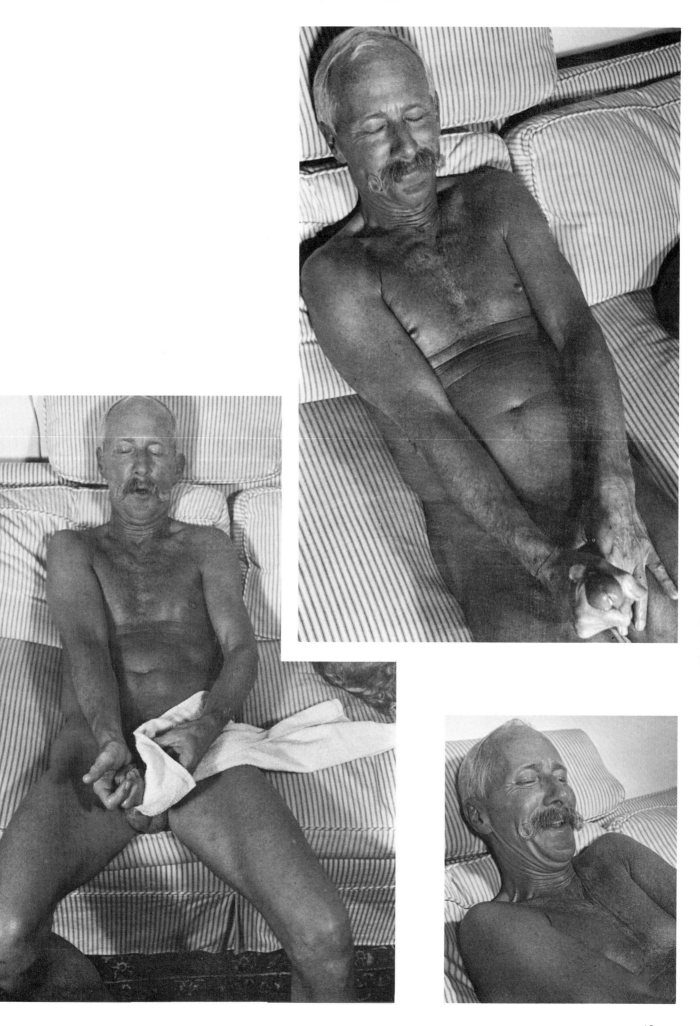

DON

I started having sex rather late. I didn't masturbate much until I was about twenty, although I had many torrid sexual feelings and fantasies in the years before.

Since then, masturbation has become a regular part of my life. The times that I love it most are after an invigorating run or energetic dancing; after being around hot, sexy men; or just before bed when I want to unwind from a busy day. I like beating off by myself or mutually with my partner.

For these self-pleasuring times I have a wealth of terrific mental pictures to help create an arousing state of mind. Many of my fantasies include jock straps—I think they are about the most erotic gear in the whole world.

After a slow scan of images, and when I feel about to come, I love to draw back to extend my pleasure even further. To do this, I touch and stroke different areas of my body or just enjoy holding my stiff cock.

When I want to come, I usually focus on special-vintage, raw sexual images of myself, my partner or other men that I have stored away in my mind and now come rushing forth. Everything merges into a warm, loving, calm blur and I feel a heightened caring for myself.

I can't imagine a day without masturbating alone or having sex with a partner. The wonderful recoiling of an orgasm keeps me nurtured, aligned and content in a very important way. I feel attractive; I have intensely expressed myself. I am the center of my attention and I applaud myself. I feel like a star.

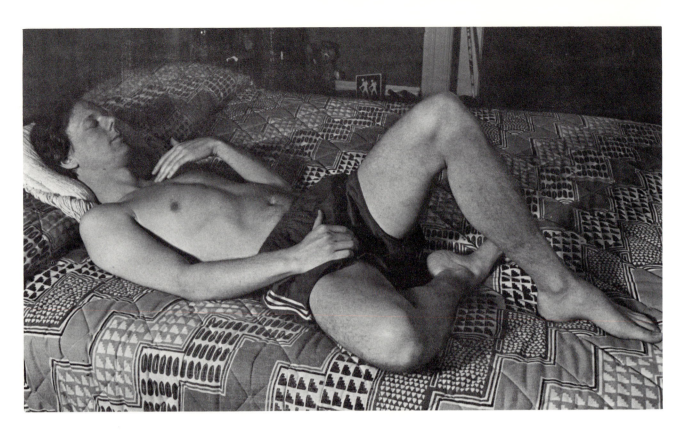

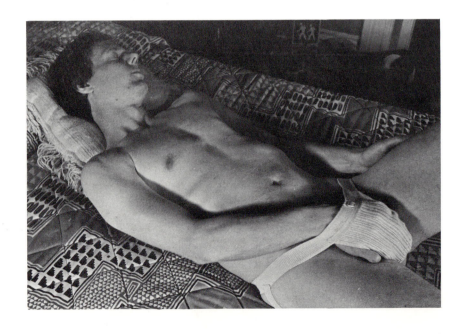

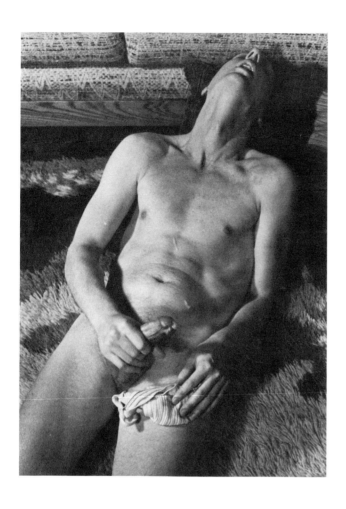 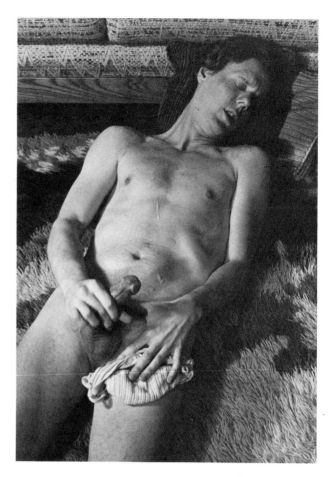

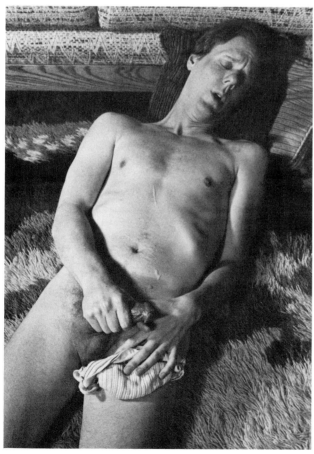 

LIM

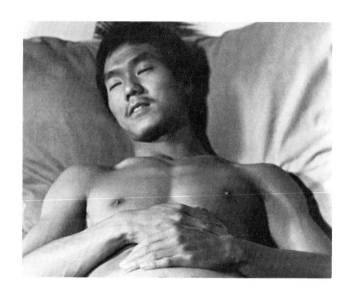

14 years ago
in a beach house
far far away
on the west coast of
Malay Peninsula
I lay with a distant cousin
on a grass mat
on a wooden floor
he was my teacher
that night was the
beginning of my love affair
with others
and myself

    Masturbation is an important expression
of my sexuality. I masturbate whether
I have a lover or not. I have to love my own
body in order to give it to someone else.
Through masturbation I learned to enjoy
myself, appreciate and respect myself.
    No matter how busy I am with things or
people I always make time for a date with
myself. Often I will cook a nice dinner, then
eat alone with candle, wine, music and
flowers. After dinner I will take a hot bath;
sometimes rose petals float on the water
with me. Sometimes I fold up paper boats
and let them float around my body. I will
tease and arouse myself for awhile. Then
I will dry myself with a soft towel and oil
and massage my body. I will touch my
chest and my neck and my thighs till my
cock throbs with the desire to be touched.
And I will play with it and play with it with
slow teasing strokes and fast strong strokes.
    Sometimes I fantasize. Sometimes I
just immerse myself in sensation and do not

fantasize at all. Sometimes I get very visual. I will stand in front of the mirror and act out my fantasy. I always moan and groan and breathe heavily. Each sound, each breath, helps me to release more and more sexual energy, and the energy forms waves, flowing, roaring, crushing and flooding my whole body.

After ejaculation I lie still for awhile. I caress my body gently and lovingly and allow myself to float away, often in a little wooden boat down the Amazon River.

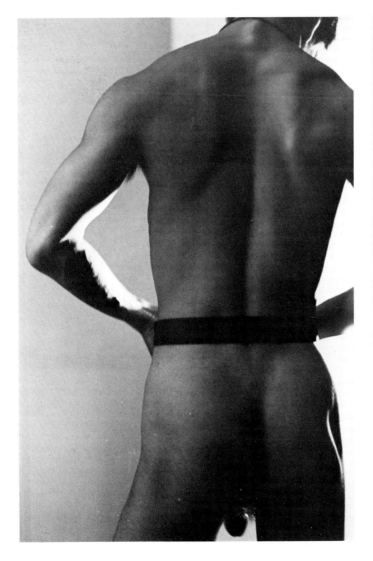 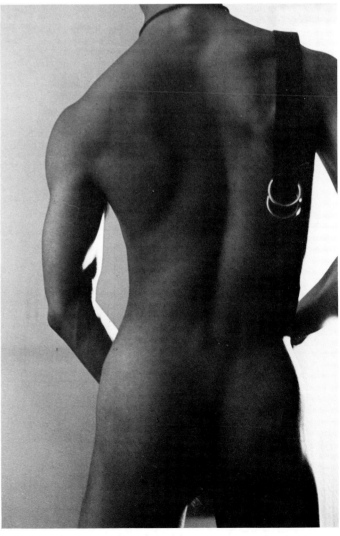

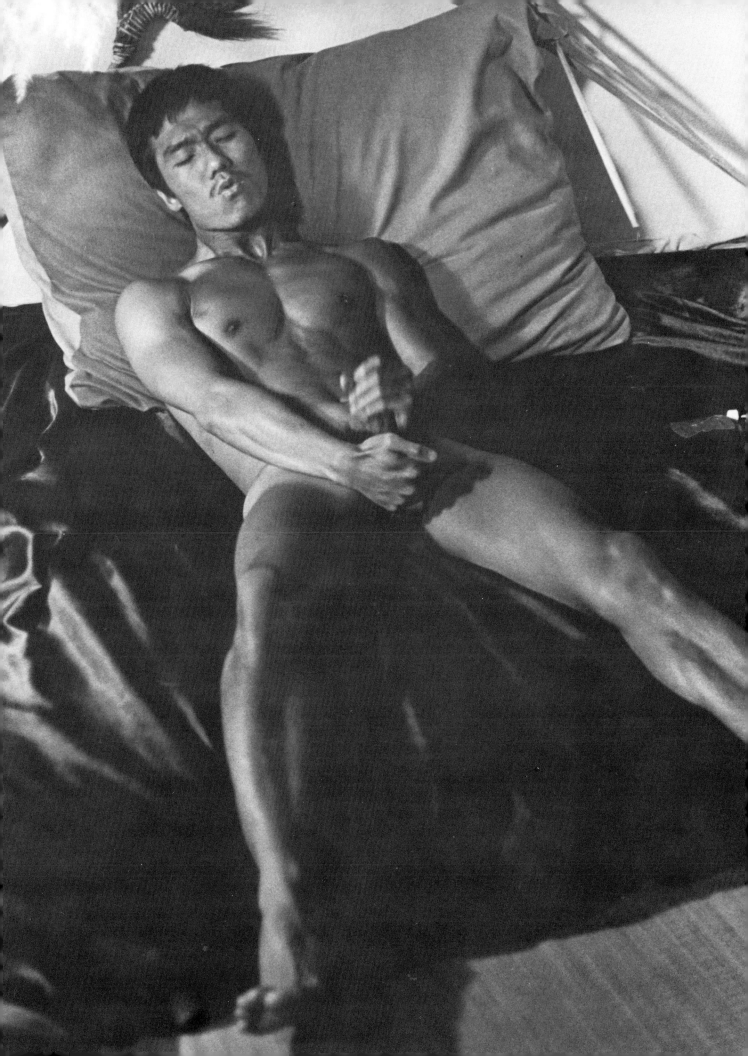

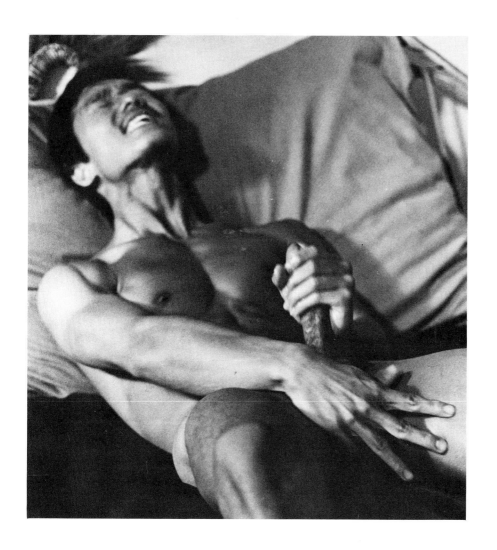

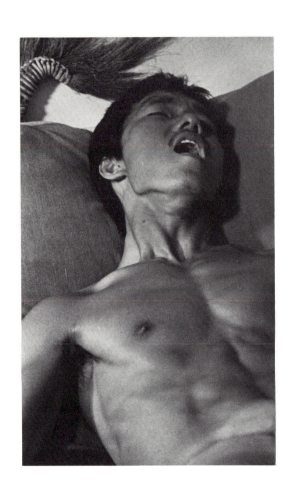

ARTHUR

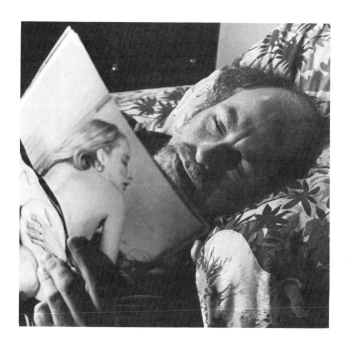

The importance of masturbation in my sex life varies, to some extent, depending on whether or not I'm involved in a steady, satisfying and committed sexual relationship. When I'm in such a relationship, I masturbate less than usual. But either way, masturbation is a constant and positive part of my sex life. I often enjoy planning ahead as to when and where I'll have a masturbation session. It's nice to look forward to it. Other times, I'm completely spontaneous, inspired by anticipation of a future encounter with a partner or seeing an attractive person.

Even if I'm in love or having lots of sex with a partner, the urge to masturbate can just hit me in response to an arousing situation. I sometimes enjoy doing it secretly with other people around. Jacking off in unexpected places and times adds excitement to the pleasure of touching myself.

The time I spend masturbating ranges from a few minutes to as long as half an hour, depending on my mood, how much I get into my fantasies, and whether I feel like playing with other parts of my body besides my cock. Occasionally, I just want a quick orgasm. Then my masturbation is focused and very intense. But I usually spend more time, beginning with slow gentle strokes which become more rapid and vigorous as excitement builds. I occasionally use saliva for lubrication. Sometimes I like to use my other hand to press against the base of my cock. The feeling of pressure increases the intensity, especially as I'm nearing an orgasm.

I almost always have fantasies while masturbating. I also enjoy sexual magazines, books and sometimes toys—such as a vibrator or dildo if I'm in the mood for anal stimulation. I like to set up my environment with all the things I want to feed my fantasies. I enjoy running through my erotic memories until an image becomes the center of my fantasy. Just a brief flash of an intriguing incident—in a far away or familiar place, long ago or recently, or a future possibility—is often all it takes to get me really turned on. Sometimes I like to play with my semen after I come or else just leave it to dry as a memento of a lovely occasion.

I enjoy masturbating with partners. But since no one else can do it quite as well as I can, I usually prefer other activities. Several times, I have masturbated myself while my partner does the same. I've also enjoyed masturbating both myself and my partner at the same time (and vice versa). In fact, ever since my first sexual experience when I was ten, masturbation in all its forms has been a thoroughly positive part of my sexuality.

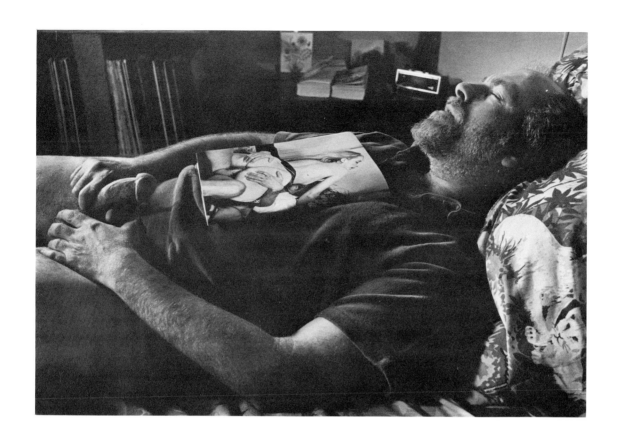

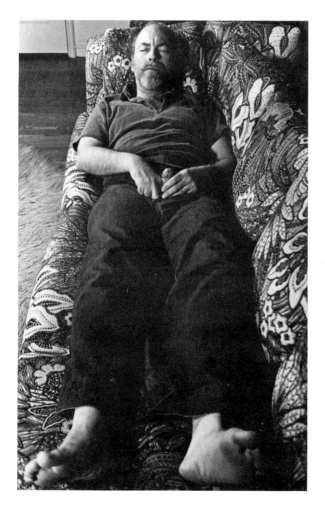

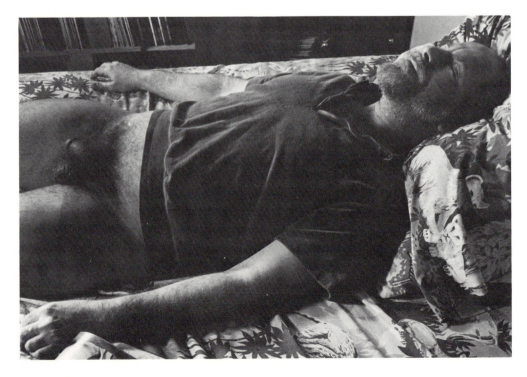

DOUG

I started jacking off when I was about 15. I liked to go skinny-dipping with friends, sometimes several at once. Some of them were already experimenting with jacking off and they'd tell me about it. I guess it was inevitable that we'd try it together. I especially liked seeing the other guys ejaculate under water.

Back then, we were very competitive. Jacking off was a contest to see who could come first and shoot the furthest. The competitive aspects faded away, though, and now I jack off only for pleasure. It's been one of my favorite forms of recreation ever since. It's not unusual for me to jack off several times a day.

It never occurred to me to feel guilty about jacking off. Sex wasn't talked about much in my family. However, there was a light, sometimes kidding atmosphere about it. I got the message it was OK to enjoy sex, even though no details were discussed.

My interest in jacking off with other guys got a boost when I was in the Navy. I loved the masculine environment. And most of the men, even the straight ones, got into "circle jerks" or jack-off sessions in the shower. A few times, the whole company (60 men) jacked off together in the dark. What a turn on that was!

I enjoy many different sexual activities, but I almost always prefer jacking off. Nobody else knows my body better than me. Timing, rhythm, the positions of my hands and body, pressure—everything— can be perfectly adjusted from moment to moment. I like long, "marathon sessions" where excitement builds very slowly, eventually leading to orgasm. Often, after a breather, I'll start all over again. I'm very visual. When I jack off alone, I usually use magazines or films to trigger my fantasies.

Jacking off is also one of my favorite sexual activities with my lover. The greatest turn-on for me is watching other guys jack off as I do it too. I have a large circle of friends now who enjoy jack-off parties. Often, a few of us get together—occasionally as many as 40 or 50—to show films, share erotic stories and jack off. It's the ultimate visual-erotic trip. Seeing a man get himself off is seeing him at his finest hour.

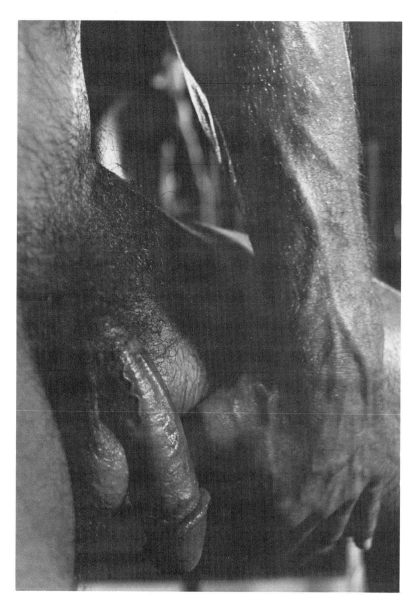

JAMES

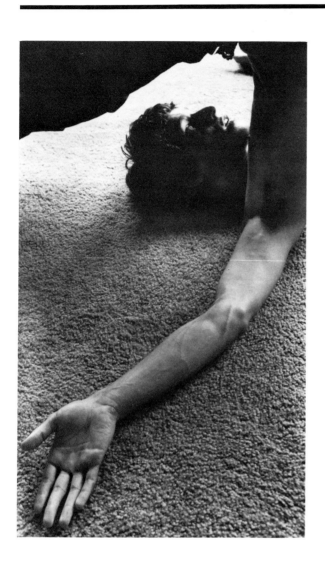

I first became aware of erections and how good they felt when I was about 9 or 10. I remember the feeling of my cock rubbing against my pants. The thought of naked bodies was also exciting to me. During the summer between seventh and eighth grades, I found a piece of "porn" in my father's dresser drawer. It was one of those pseudo-psychological treatises that included hot case histories of people with different sexual "perversions." I then started deliberately rubbing my cock and touching other parts of my body. I can still remember how strong the sexual tension in my whole body was. After I experienced my first orgasm, masturbation became a passionate interest with me, and it still is.

Masturbation is a very important part of my life and the most important part of my sex life. I need a lot of privacy and my favorite way of spending time alone is self-pleasuring. That includes cleaning my house, fixing myself dinner, lighting candles, placing pillows in front of my mirror—getting the place so I can feel comfortable in it. For me, creating the right environment is a ritual that is an integral part of the entire self-pleasuring experience.

Yoga plays a large part in most of my masturbation sessions. I use the breathing, relaxation and stretching to get into my body so I can really feel. Tension blocks my sensual feelings and yoga helps release that tension.

I often take breaks. I will explore one fantasy for a while. Then I'll stop, go get a glass of water and sit around until another fantasy hits me. The time after I have an orgasm is really important to me too. I pay attention to how I feel—centered, alive and

I have a sense of completion all over my body.

There is not a clear division between my sexual/sensual life and the rest of my life. I am a sexual person and this energy is in everything I do. It is wonderful that I can satisfy myself on an ongoing basis, that I can be self-sufficient. Being sexual with a partner is great too, but it is no substitute for being sexual with myself.

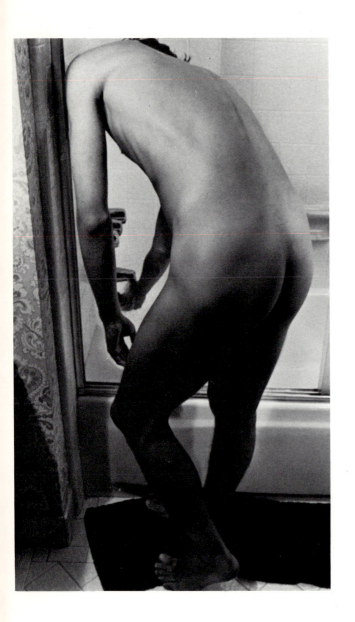

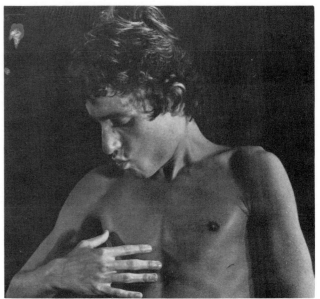
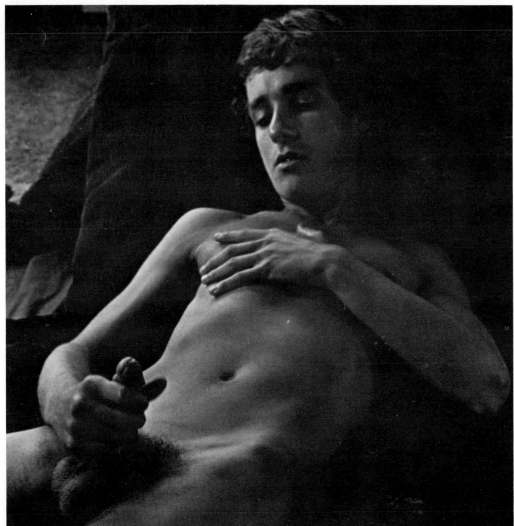

FREDDIE

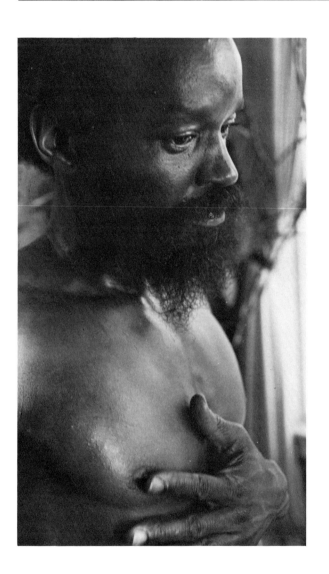

I was thirteen or fourteen when I had my first masturbation experience. In those days I did it just because it felt good.

As I grew older, there was a change both in my masturbation pattern and in my motivation for doing it. Now I masturbate sometimes for fun and sometimes for enrichment.

"Fun" masturbation is the term I use to describe playing with myself when I am with a friend or talking with someone on the phone. The telephone fantasy is especially nice for me.

I also do what I call "enrichment" masturbation. I always do that alone. I touch and massage all parts of my body. I pay close attention to my own responses, to the physical changes in my body, and I learn more about myself each time.

If I am working long hours, or during periods when I have a regular sexual partner, I masturbate by myself less frequently. Whether I am masturbating a lot or a little, whether I do it for "fun" or for "enrichment," it always gives me a great deal of enjoyment.

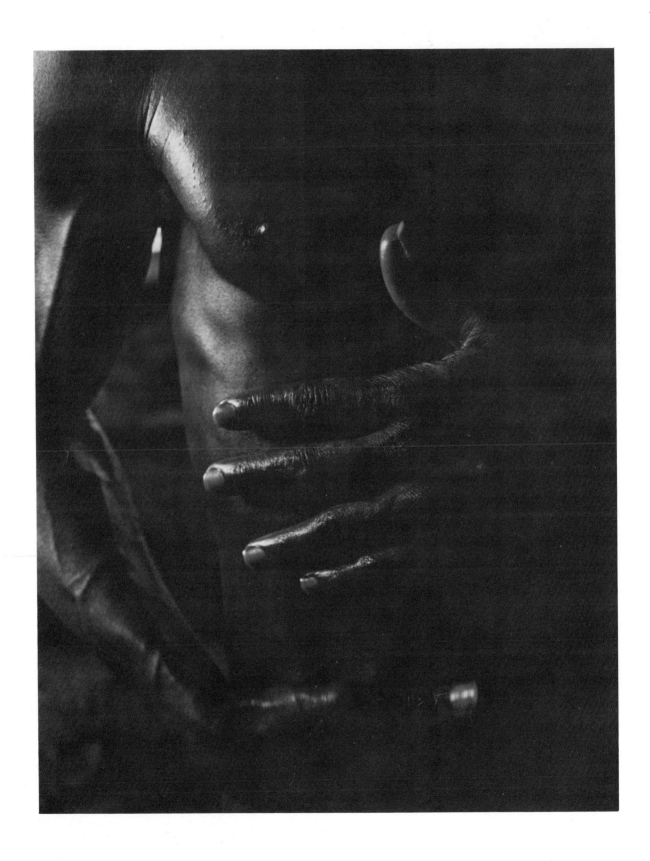

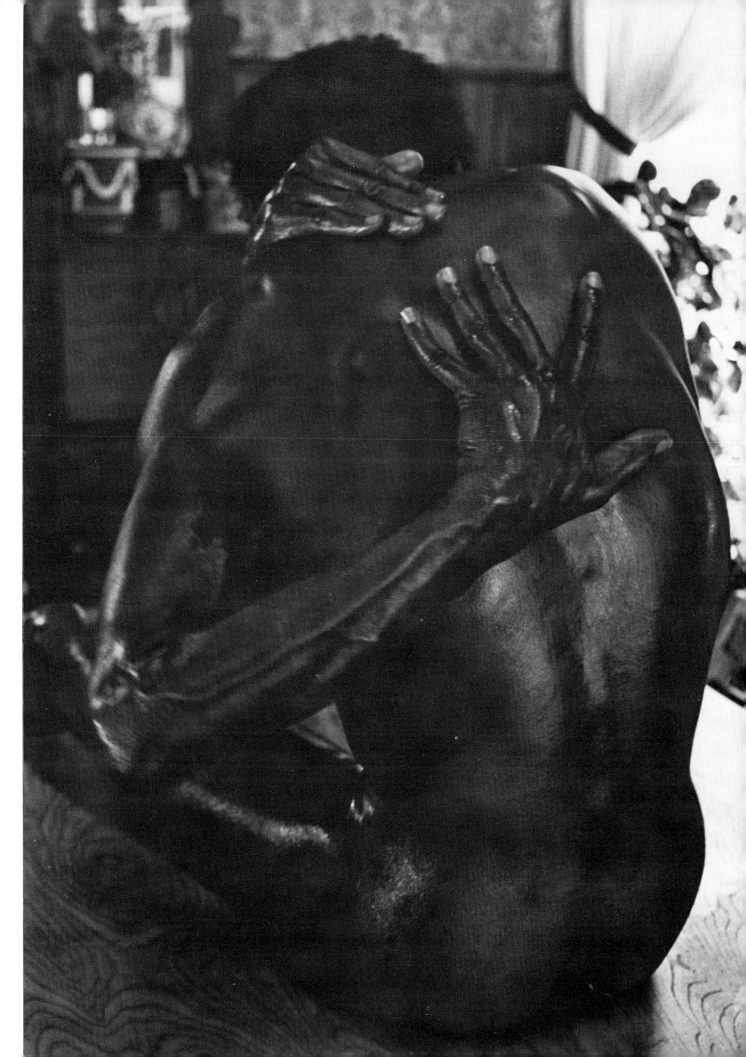

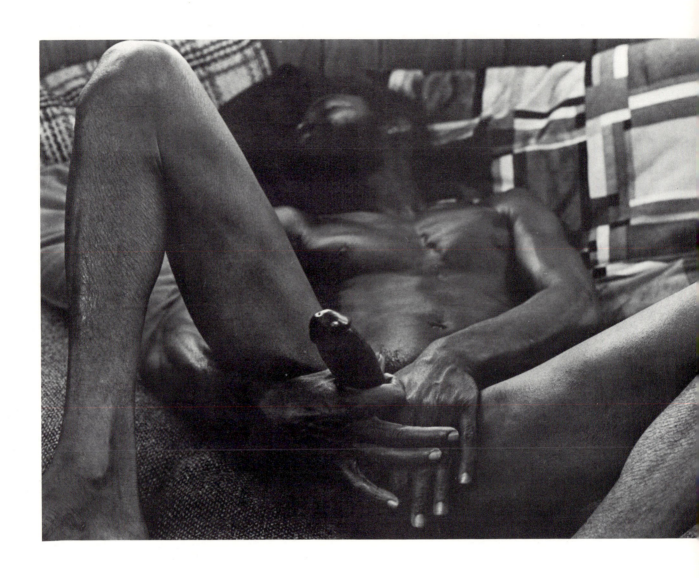

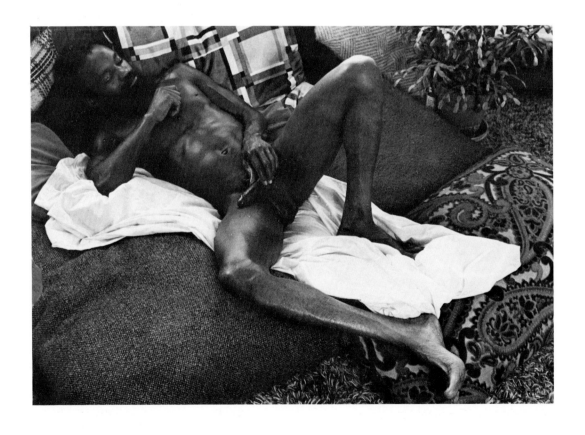

THE PSYCHOLOGY
OF MALE SELF-SEXUALITY

Prior to the publication of the first Kinsey report in the late forties, respected, responsible, in fact brilliant people were in the habit of blaming virtually every conceivable human ailment on masturbation. They did this, in part, through a simple error in logic, which found fertile ground in the moral climate of the times: since almost everyone with problems masturbates, they reasoned, therefore masturbation must *cause* the problems. What was so shocking about the Kinsey data was the discovery that masturbation (far from being the solitary vice of the lonely, sick and depraved) is practiced with widely variable frequency by members of every group, whether sick or healthy, satisfied or miserable. Had they been so inclined, early investigators could just as well have concluded, using the same faulty logic, that masturbation "causes" creativity, the capacity for love, success in business or anything else.

During the next two decades, the leading voices in the study of human sexuality, following Kinsey's lead, were suggesting that masturbation was not only benign, but could be beneficial. Now, masturbation is often recommended by sex counselors and psychotherapists for sexual enhancement and to help their clients resolve sexual problems. Within three decades of Kinsey's studies, expert opinion about masturbation had done nearly a complete turnaround.

Needless to say, this has been a difficult transition for many people to make. Commonly, positive views of masturbation have been laid over traditional negative attitudes like a veneer, resulting in confusion or ambivalence. Often there is a battle between what one knows (intellectually) and what one feels about masturbation. In addition, there is usually another conflict between information recently acquired and more deeply ingrained ideas about the functions and meanings of sex. In psychology, for example, most of the dominant theories (our yardsticks for mental health) are derived from models of sexual health inescapably biased against masturbation. Integrating new data, insights and feelings about masturbation requires a sweeping conceptual shift.

Changes in how one feels about masturbation often require alternative ways to *think* about it. The following material is intended to serve as a catalyst for fresh ideas about self-sexuality. The general per-

spective as well as specific concepts have grown out of my experience with hundreds of men with whom I have had contact as therapist, sex counselor and teacher. Some of the men were having sexual problems; others were not. Some explicitly wanted to explore self-sexuality from the beginning; others unexpectedly moved in this direction as part of a larger process of sexual self-exploration.

While available statistical data could certainly use updating and expanding, I am concerned here with different kinds of questions. How, specifically, does a person with a long history of discomfort about masturbation develop more positive attitudes? What factors are most likely to get in the way? What unquestioned ideas and convictions may have to be acknowledged and confronted? What new ideas, if any, will replace the old ones? And what impact might these changes have on one's overall sexuality?

When discussing erotic stimulation which a person consciously and deliberately gives to himself (alone or in the presence of a partner), I use the terms self-sexuality, masturbation and autoeroticism interchangeably. Slang terms such as jerk, jack, beat or whack off are probably used more commonly by men. However, these terms are not used here because they connote one type of self-stimulation: genitally-focused, vigorous and usually rapid. This connotation is far too limited.

THE USES OF SELF-SEXUALITY

The widespread tendency to devalue masturbation prevents many people from recognizing the subtle complexities of self-sexual activities. Not all masturbation is the same; people use it for a variety of different purposes. The desire for pleasure is, of course, the motivator behind most autoerotic behavior. But the amount and kind of pleasure which one experiences during a masturbation session depends, to a large extent, on the interaction of two variables: 1) the reason(s) for doing it, and 2) how effectively the experience serves the desired function. In some instances, the greater the conscious understanding of what one hopes to gain, the better the chances that the activity will be highly pleasurable. This is not the case, however, when something is expected of masturbation which it cannot, by nature, deliver. In these cases, a clearer recognition of the *limitations* of self-sexuality should result in a gradual shift in expectations.

Any attempt to categorize individuals according to their reasons for masturbating is, of course, doomed (and pointless). Almost every masturbation session has more than one function. And the reasons for doing it may change as excitement builds and self-consciousness recedes. Nonetheless, most men who look closely will discern a striking consistency in their reasons for masturbating from one time to the next. Usually, one or two uses predominate while others are deemphasized or ignored.

For purposes of self-exploration, it is helpful to recognize the divergent uses of self-sexuality. It is important to keep in mind that, in actual practice, the distinctions between these may not be so clear. The functions which most men seem to acknowledge and understand will be discussed first, then those of which fewer men are aware.

Substitute for a Partner

Masturbation is almost universally recognized as something men do when their regular sexual partner isn't available or when they have no partner(s). Ironically, while this is perhaps the most common reason men masturbate, it is also the function that masturbation usually serves *least* effectively. Solo-sex can provide some of the excitement and pleasure of an encounter with a desired partner. However, when masturbation is used as a substitute for partner sex, it almost always feels like a second-best version of "the real thing." This is hardly surprising. When any activity is consistently compared to another more-favored activity, the substitute activity will drop in value and the more-favored activity will increase in value. This is intensified when the more-favored activity is unavailable. In fact, with few exceptions, the more a man uses masturbation as a substitute for partner sex, the less he will value it. Occasionally, using masturbation this way also results in devaluation of future sexual encounters with partners when these encounters fail to match expectations based on masturbation fantasies.

Stress Reduction and Relaxation

People frequently masturbate to relieve the tensions of the day and/or to help them go to sleep. Self-sexuality used this way tends to be relatively rapid (often less than five minutes). This is because the heightened excitement which precedes orgasm temporarily *increases* tension. The tension-discharging orgasm is clearly the goal and most are in a hurry to get there. To facilitate speedy tension-reduction, many people establish habitual or ritualized masturbation patterns (e.g. always the same way, position, place or time). "Compulsive" masturbation, in which a person feels driven to do it even if he doesn't feel like it, is, essentially, a tension-reducing strategy that doesn't work. More accurately, it is no match for an extremely high level of stress. For relatively mild stress, however, masturbation is an effective antidote with no negative side effects (see Rusty's statement, page 19).

Fantasy Catalyst

Most men fantasize, at least some of the time, during masturbation. The fantasies serve several different purposes. When masturbation is a substitute for partner sex, the partner can be included via mental imagery, which boosts the erotic charge of the solo-sex session. This can be done by "replaying," and perhaps embellishing, exciting past sexual events; by imagining future sexual encounters; or by exploring erotic events which could never actually occur (see Billy's statement, page 13).

Sometimes fantasy is used initially to generate excitement, after which attention is focused more on bodily sensations. For some people, this progression is reversed. That is, touch-induced arousal generates the fantasies which are the primary focus of the experience. For some, fantasy is a way of exploring activities one would actually like to do. For others, fantasies provide a safe way to enjoy activities which, if actually experienced, would be dangerous, repulsive or frightening. With or without erotic materials such as books, magazines or movies, masturbation is probably the most popular, but certainly not the only context for exploring erotic mental images.

"Equipment" Check and Workout

Men sometimes masturbate in order to check and maintain their sexual responses and/or to give themselves the good feelings associated with a physical workout. Heeding the old adage, "use it or lose it," some people masturbate out of a belief that doing so will contribute to life-long sexual responsiveness (a belief which appears to contain an element of truth). In the context of the current fitness boom, masturbation is sometimes included in an individual's health-promoting routine (see Don's statement, page 45).

Self-sexual activities can serve all of these functions quite well. However, the workout value of masturbation is obviously limited when a person spends only a few moments doing it or restricts deep breathing and free movement. Occasionally, when self-sexuality is used by a person concerned about sexual problems, his masturbation becomes a test or a performance. To the extent that he fears "failure" (being unable to get an erection, slow down a rapid ejaculation, ejaculate at all, etc.) his activities will become steadily less pleasurable until, ultimately, his worst fears will probably be confirmed. Masturbation does not work any better than partner sex when we are struggling to prove or disprove something.

Recreation

For some men, self-sexuality is a readily available, free, safe and highly rewarding form of recreation or play. Since it is not viewed as a substitute for anything, it can be enjoyed for what it has to offer without comparison to any other pleasurable activity. Understandably, masturbation-as-recreation is enjoyed especially by those who also enjoy other solitary activities. Those who are bored or distressed by their own company may have trouble comprehending how anyone could enjoy playing alone. Those who do enjoy their own company tend to be the most innovative and experimental masturbators. There are, however, many people who thoroughly enjoy playing alone but do not particularly enjoy masturbation. Since those who do enjoy it are usually in no hurry to get it over with, they tend to spend more time and often describe themselves as one of their best sex partners.

Expression of Male Camaraderie

In spite of strong prohibitions against it, a surprisingly large number of men have masturbated with other men, especially during adolescence. They show or tell each other how, compete with one another and sometimes have group masturbation sessions ("circle jerks"). Very frequently, masturbation among two or more males occurs without the participants touching each other at all. Although these activities are technically homosexual, the common idea that they are part of an adolescent "homosexual phase" clouds their true significance.

It is true that for some gay adolescents, masturbating with other males is the only available means of exploring their erotic preference. In fact, most gay men find these experiences so exciting that they include them permanently in their sexual preference system, and some continue group masturbation into adulthood (see Doug's statement, page 63).

Most young men who masturbate together are *not* exploring homosexuality. Many fear that masturbating with other males might mean they are gay and are hence reluctant to do it very much, talk about it or even think about it. However, when, as adults, they are pressed to think about what they got out of it, most discover that masturbating together was primarily a means of reinforcing each other's sexualness and bolstering their masculinity. In this sense, male-male masturbation is similar to other forms of male camaraderie which have the same functions: teaching each other about expected social-sexual behavior, passing along the myth that the phallus is the essence of sexuality, sharing attitudes and expectations about women and women's sexuality, and establishing a sense of independence from family. Being in the company of other males (which, for some, includes masturbating together) is a crucial aspect of male sexual learning.

Body Exploration

Although a great many men initially use masturbation as a means of becoming familiar with their bodies and sexual responses, this is usually limited to the genital area. Other parts of the body are largely ignored. Even genital awareness recedes considerably when self-stimulation patterns become habitual. Especially when orgasm is the overriding goal, detailed awareness of the process leading to orgasm may be virtually absent.

In recent years, more sex counselors are recognizing the value of bodily self-exploration for enhancing both private and shared sexual encounters. One of the most effective ways to discover body zones responsive to touch and the most pleasurable types of touch is to explore in private. Sexual self-exploration can also be used to eroticize areas of the body not previously experienced as erogenous (see Don's statement, page 27).

Self-sexuality can be used to alter general erotic responses as well. For example, most men can learn to reduce the urge to ejaculate quickly with a partner by first slowing down their responses during masturbation. A man can also learn to relax during sexual encounters by first learning to relax alone. He can also use self-sexuality to help him develop a more sensual, less genitally-focused and non-performance-oriented approach to sex with partners.

Self-Affirmation

A good sexual experience leaves one feeling affirmed and validated. Yet affirmation need not always come from another person. A satisfying masturbation session can be an opportunity for self-affirmation too. Just as with partner sex, people sometimes initiate solo-sex activities specifically to meet their need for validation.

Masturbation can be used to affirm one's overall worth. But more often, the affirmation is specifically related to one's sexual desirability. Masturbation can be used to get out of a bad mood or to celebrate a good mood. For example, many men report that some of their most memorable masturbation sessions occur soon after a satisfying encounter with a partner or after some other validating, but non-sexual chronically preoccupied with self. Why? Not because he loves himself too much, but because he is deeply alienated from his inner world. He falls in love with his reflections in other people because he does not see, accept and love himself. Self-love is a major part of the "cure" for narcissism, not the cause. Coupled with self knowledge, self-love makes it possible to recognize and care for another person as a separate, independent being. This recognition is essential for intimacy.

When a person always places other people's feelings and needs ahead of his own, he is exhibiting a behavior pattern sometimes called the *Nice Person Syndrome*. Because people who behave this way display an intense sensitivity to what other people want, they are usually thought of as exceptionally non-narcissistic. This idea, too, is erroneous. In actuality, the Nice Person is unable or unwilling to differentiate his own feelings from those of a partner. In sex, the amount of pleasure expressed by the partner determines the value of the encounter. The Nice Person Syndrome involves much more than getting pleasure from giving (which is an authentic source of eroticism and joy). When operating strongly, this pattern leads to the same blurring of interpersonal boundaries which characterizes narcissism and usually springs from the same source: self-alienation (combined, in most Nice People, with heavy doses of guilt and unconscious resentment).

It should be noted that a certain amount of blurring of psychic boundaries naturally occurs in the course of intense romantic relationships and other times when we feel particularly needy and incomplete. This becomes problematic only when there is a *chronic* inability to experience oneself and another as separate persons.

Traditional psychological theories, especially Freudian psychology and many of its derivatives, assume a link between narcissism and one's level of interest in masturbation, because both are believed to be immature. However, there is absolutely no evidence that people who are uncertain about their psychic boundaries masturbate or have partner sex any more or less than any other group. Instead, self-alienated people, while exhibiting the same range of sexual preferences as everyone else, usually do not feel satisfied by anything they do because they lack the internal "home base" from which to enjoy it. Conversely, those whose sense of self *is* clearly and comfortably defined are far more likely to experience whatever they choose to do, including masturbation, as self-expressive and affirming.

Limitations of the Male Role

Every man must contend with the ever-present pressure to strive toward the masculine ideal roles implicit in his culture. He probably won't meet the ideals, and he may even reject them; but he must relate to them nonetheless, because they are too powerful to ignore. Although informed men no longer feel that masturbation is abusive to their bodies, many feel that self-sexuality *is* somehow abusive to their masculinity. Most men feel that *Real Men* get women (or other men) to meet their sexual needs and that taking care of one's own needs constitutes, at least to some degree, a failure.

More often than not, the sense of failure is concentrated on the importance of power in stereotypically masculine role models. The Real Man hunts, seduces and eventually overcomes and dominates his sex partners, all the while remaining unruffled. His central interest is supposed to be to *penetrate* the world and especially his sex partners. His penis is thought of as a weapon of sorts (e.g. a "violator" or "love pistol"). Even the word penetration, still often used synonomously with intercourse, connotes struggle and resistance. If there is no actual or fantasized resistance, it is only possible for a penis to *enter* an orifice; an act of penetration requires a barrier.

To the extent that this is a man's sexual ideal, self-sexuality will probably be devalued. And to the extent that acted-out power interchanges have become necessary for sexual arousal, he will be unable to enjoy self-sexuality even if he'd like to.

A central theme in virtually all ideal images of masculinity is the avoidance and suppression of qualities considered feminine—and therefore weak. The harder a man tries to live up to this standard, however, the more intense becomes his irrational fear of femininity. Sexually, such a man will probably feel compelled to remain constantly active, to initiate and choreograph encounters and accept total responsibility for their "success." Most likely, he'll find it difficult to lie back, surrender control and become receptive to his partner's touch. He may also find it difficult to be receptive to his own touch during masturbation. Ironically, the same masculine ideals which encourage him to have as many sexual experiences as possible, simultaneously limit his capacity to enjoy them fully.

The fear of expressing qualities considered feminine is closely related to another fear—*homophobia*, the irrational fear of homosexuality. It is almost universally believed that gay male sexuality represents womanliness in a man and vice versa (even though a close look at gay male sexual behavior patterns reveals that gay male sexuality is, first and foremost, *male* sexuality). Men who feel that there is something feminine about self-sexuality also tend to believe that there is something homosexual about it. For example, a large number of men who were asked to consider being photographed for this book immediately replied, "No, I'm not gay," assuming that the enjoyment of masturbation has something to do with one's sexual orientation (which it does not). In part, this assumption stems from the inevitable fact that male masturbation involves the enjoyment of a male body and a penis—at least on the level of overt behavior. However, considering the enjoyment of one's own body a homosexual act suggests pervasive anxiety about one's sexual orientation. Such concerns are fostered by popular masculine ideals which call for a strict polarization of sex roles. Whether a man is straight, gay or bisexual, attachment to these ideals results in a narrowing of his behavioral repertoire, and a restriction of his capacity for pleasure, whether alone or with a partner.

Loneliness/Fear of Loneliness

No matter how good it is, masturbation in private cannot meet one's need for intimate interpersonal contact. In fact, when a person is feeling lonely—particularly if this feeling is persistent—masturbation can intensify his sense of isolation even further. Even those with regular intimate contacts can feel lonely. This can happen when one's relationships do not measure up to his fantasies of total involvement and boundless mutual understanding. Others live with a nagging fear of being abandoned, which can increase the closer one gets to another person. And if masturbation is believed to be a form of "cheating," doing it may activate fear of reprisals and eventual abandonment.

Everyone feels lonely at times, especially during periods of personal transition and/or rapid social change. Sometimes, emerging awareness of one's essential aloneness is soothed by a loving encounter with oneself. However, self-sexuality can also function as an unwelcome reminder of one's separateness and will then be unpleasant. Masturbation can especially be a trigger for lonely feelings when early self-sexual behavior is intertwined with blocked desire for sexual contact, which is so often the case during adolescence.

Whatever the source of loneliness, it cannot be completely avoided; it's an integral part of being human. Paradoxically, facing and accepting one's aloneness appears to provide the most secure foundation for enduring and satisfying relationships. Intimacy becomes more enjoyable—and less threatening—when its limitations are acknowledged.

Fantasy Blockages

Since fantasy plays an important role in most men's masturbation, anything which blocks the free flow of fantasy can disrupt the enjoyment of self-sexuality. Some men involved in ongoing, especially monogomous, relationships, feel that fantasy images of women/men other than their regular partner constitute violations of their commitment (see Marvin's statement, page 5). Fantasy may then be carefully controlled to avoid the spontaneous appearance of forbidden people. Eventually, this can generate so much confict that enjoyment of masturbation becomes impossible.

Others are disturbed by fantasy images considered "sick" or otherwise unacceptable. Some concerns focus on the fantasy characters (for example, a parent or other family member, someone of a different sex than usual, someone younger than the age of consent or the boss's wife). For others, the primary concern is not *who* is in the fantasy, but *what* activities are imagined. The vast majority of these fantasies are those in which erotic charge is generated by simple or complex scenes based on extreme power roles ("sado-masochistic" fantasies). To protect themselves from disturbing fantasies, many men try to shut out fantasy altogether and often avoid masturbation, seeing it as the "breeding ground" for unacceptable thoughts.

No matter what the source of blocked fantasy, suppression rarely works. The stronger the attempts to suppress them, the more persistent the troublesome images become. In many instances, fantasy images which, if left unrestricted, would have been fleeting, are inflated by attempted suppression into full-blown preoccupations. It is far more conducive to sexual enjoyment—though not always easily done—to differentiate the realm of fantasy from behavior. It is pointless (as well as difficult or impossible) to apply to fantasy those values and limitations which can readily be applied to what one actually does. People frequently have fantasies which they have no desire or need to act upon. Yet there are times when fantasy signals a desire for actual experimentation. In these instances, the only effective means of unblocking fantasy is to structure safe, consensual and self-affirming ways to roleplay fantasies alone or during sexual encounters. The ability to do this can be developed even by those who initially feel self-conscious and cannot abandon themselves to the roleplaying.

Sexual Conservation Concerns

A widespread notion—with a long tradition in both Eastern and Western thought—is the idea that each of us is endowed with a fixed amount of sexual energy. Although this belief is rarely expressed directly these days, worries about wasting or using up sexual energy are still quite common. While it is now known that the supply of semen is constantly replenished, men often feel vague concerns about running out if they "overdo it."

In addition, men sometimes report a loss of psychic energy following ejaculation. This is why practitioners of Tantric Yoga seek to inhibit ejaculation during orgasm. They are convinced that by doing so, psychic energy is retained. Based on a similar belief, some men try to save up sexual energy by avoiding ejaculation for as long as possible. They believe their orgasm is more intense when they finally allow themselves to have one. Ideas like these contribute to negative comparisons of self-sexuality and partner sex. If we can only have so much sex, we had better choose carefully. Some men simply will not masturbate if they hope to have sex with a partner any time soon.

It is true that most people feel a temporary loss of sexual interest following orgasm. This may last from a few minutes, to days, or weeks. To what extent this is due to physiology and how much it is the result of preference or expectation is impossible to determine. Each man's body functions differently. His expectations, however, are often more influential than he realizes. If a man expects to feel a loss of energy following orgasm, then that's what he will feel. If he expects masturbation to diminish his interest in partner sex, then it probably will.

For many men, there appears to be little or no relationship between sexual interest and the time span since the last orgasm. Emotional state, the intensity of external erotic stimuli, and the quality of interaction with a partner affect the level of interest far more. There is also tremendous variation in the amounts of sexual tension which people find pleasurable. Some people have a very low tolerance for erotic tension and, therefore, seek frequent orgasms. Others enjoy long periods of sexual abstinence, not because they are "saving it up," but because they enjoy a sense of heightened erotic sensitivity during these times.

Loss of Naughtiness

Since most people first masturbate in the context of ambivalence, it is not surprising that many learn to associate the enjoyment of self-sexuality with feelings of naughtiness, furtivenes, getting away with something or violating the rules. Popular adjectives used to describe sexual behavior such as raunchy, sleazy or trashy reflect the same association. This tie between eroticism and naughtiness greatly increases excitement for a large number of people. Many adults are only vaguely (if at all) aware that they *like* to feel naughty when they masturbate. The idea that masturbation can be openly enjoyed without guilt may be unwelcome and, at least initially, anti-erotic. This same phenomenon commonly occurs with other forms of sexual behavior.

One way to cope with this is to maintain the sense of naughtiness one desires by focusing on fantasies (or behavior) which enhance the feeling of naughtiness. (This is commonly done by using pornography, much of which capitalizes on people's enjoyment of naughty feelings.) Another approach involves gradually allowing bodily sensations and feelings other than naughtiness to become increasingly significant erotically. This cannot be done through "will power" or suppression. Instead, relaxed experimentation is most likely to lead to modifications of erotic preference. Of course, a person can use both approaches, sometimes enjoying naughtiness, sometimes enjoying other fantasies and sensations.

Lack of Privacy

Most people in our culture consider privacy to be desirable, if not essential, for sexual enjoyment. The strength of one's desire for privacy appears to depend mostly on early childhood experiences in the family. The need for privacy is particularly intense in families where nudity and sexual activities occur not only in private, but also under the cloak of secrecy. In some families, being completely alone, or alone with another person automatically has sexual overtones which may generate suspicion and/or sexual excitement, depending on who the participants are. When sex is not discussed in a household, whatever the relationship of the members, awareness of sexual activity may make people vaguely uncomfortable and uncertain how to respond. For example, one may pretend not to notice sexual sounds in the next room.

Even household members who can accept sexual activities with a partner may be completely unwilling to acknowledge self-sexuality. In fact, many adults, especially those who are married, continue the pattern of furtive masturbation which they began as adolescents. Sneaking a quick masturbation session in the shower or when nobody is home may result in an orgasm and a sense of naughty excitement; but it is not conducive to leisurely enjoyment.

A great many people living with sexual partners abandon self-sexuality altogether, either because they think their partner would be upset if he/she found out about it or because the logistics of keeping it secret seem hopelessly complex. Some of these people will insist that they don't want to or don't "need" to masturbate when, in actuality, finding privacy has simply become too problematic.

When privacy is important to a person, he almost always can find times and locations for himself, although he may have to be assertive to do so. It is much easier to arrange for the privacy necessary to enjoy masturbation, however, when the desire for privacy is freed from the burden of maintaining absolute secrecy. Then one can request (or insist on) privacy without feeling furtive.

Fear of Dependency

A few people avoid masturbation specifically because they are concerned about becoming "hooked" on autoerotic activities and therefore less interested in, or responsive to, sexual partners. Although it appears to be relatively rare, this does occasionally occur. Some men become exclusively focused on masturbation because they fear sex with partners. For these men, a reduction of fear or an increase in willingness to take interpersonal risks will almost always result in a rapid and automatic rearrangement of sexual priorities, and a disappearance of the dependency.

Another form of dependency on masturbation involves a conditioned attachment to specific kinds of stimulation. A few men become so attached to one type of stimulation that unless it is duplicated exactly with a partner, they are unable to respond at all, or else they find it difficult or impossible to ejaculate. Once such an attachment develops, attempts to avoid masturbation are of no value. The solution involves gradual expansion of autoerotic flexibility combined with the development of skills in asking partners for the type of stimulation one likes.

ENHANCING SELF-SEXUALITY

There are many practical steps which can be taken to initiate or expand enjoyment of sexual self-stimulation. The following suggestions have been helpful to many men and women. No two people use the suggestions exactly the same way; there is no recipe for autoerotic pleasure. Most of the suggestions are stated generally to avoid restricting spontaneity and creativity. Even so, many people feel anything but spontaneous the first time (or several times) they experiment. A little awkwardness is to be expected. In addition, one or more of the self-sexuality inhibitors are often most strongly felt in the early phases of experimentation. When this happens, it can be immensely helpful to discuss one's feelings with a friend or lover, perhaps as she or he is exploring self-sexuality too.

Turning sexual possibilities into new demands can diminish the value of any sexual experimentation. Most of the sexual ideals popular in our society are overwhelmingly performance-oriented. Old myths about the value of sexual purity or abstinence have been replaced by new myths about sexual perfection. We are supposed to be totally versatile, free of all

"hang-ups" and inhibitions. These days, it isn't unusual for people to experiment with new forms of sexual enjoyment not so much because they want to, but mostly because they feel they must (to please a partner or bolster their image as a sexual sophisticate).

Feelings of obligation are hardly ever effective motivators for sexual enhancement because they create pressure and, in most cases, reduce the capacity for pleasure. Self-sexual experimentation, therefore, is best done only when and if a person envisions discovering something useful and pleasurable *for himself*. To do this, it is necessary to keep in mind that no particular sexual activity is required for a satisfying sex life. On the other hand, expectations play an important role in determining which sexual activities and situations will be pleasurable and which will not. Especially in the area of self-sexuality, most people are primed to expect very little indeed. It would be good if we could experiment without filtering our experiences through any pre-existing expectations. Unfortunately, however, even this is unattainable. About the best we can do is be aware of our expectations and risk altering them in the light of new information.

Almost all self-sexual enhancement involves at least some "deritualization." This means deliberately doing things a little differently than usual. The more predictable a person's masturbation patterns have been, the more he can expect to gain by becoming more flexible.

Places. Sometimes it is enjoyable to masturbate in a different place than usual: in another room, outdoors, in a car or other unexpected place (see Billy's and Arthur's statements, pages 13 and 59). Altering one's usual environment for masturbation, even in little ways, can also make the experience more special.

Times. Most men masturbate just before going to sleep. This is why many are convinced that masturbation makes them tired. But solo-sex can also energize, creating a state of relaxed readiness for action when it's done at the beginning of the day or during a midday break (see Marvin's statement, page 5). In fact, any departure from one's usual time of masturbation can add interest to the experience.

Forms. It's not unusual for men to become so habituated to one type of touch that involuntary changes (such as an injury of one's usual masturbation hand) seem to render masturbation impossible. A few men have conditioned themselves to respond to a highly specialized form of stimulation to such an extent that they find it difficult to respond to partners.

In less dramatic ways, most men have restricted the ways they pleasure themselves. Therefore, expanding one's usual self-stimulation repertoire (for example, other hand, with/without lubrication, faster or slower, new positions) can help increase the enjoyment of self-sexuality.

Initially, masturbating in new ways may feel strange or less exciting. When this happens, some people are tempted to revert to old, familiar patterns without giving themselves a chance to adapt to the new sensations. Familiar masturbation patterns should not be suppressed or avoided while experimenting. Instead, new forms of self-stimulation are more easily integrated when they are included as supplements to the old favorites. Also, since high levels of excitement are reinforcing, it is more effective to introduce new forms of stimulation when one is already aroused.

Developing self-sexual flexibility requires the willingness to experiment as well as the ability to say no to one's internalized demands, expectations or habits. Since any often-repeated behavior may become habituated, autoerotic enhancement sometimes includes deciding *not* to masturbate on those occasions when the urge comes from habit rather than genuine desire. This can be tricky, however, when a decision not to masturbate converges with morally-charged negative messages about sex in general or self-sexuality in particular. Since so many men begin masturbating in a state of conflict, freely-chosen abstinence may be difficult or impossible to distinguish from suppression.

Internal battles over whether or not to masturbate—while usually limiting enjoyment—may also generate intense excitement. Ambivalence can be an effective aphrodisiac. Therefore, some people are reluctant to defuse their struggle with masturbation, fearing a loss of arousal. If a drop in excitement does occur, it is virtually always temporary. When auto-erotic activities are chosen (or set aside) purely on the basis of desire (or lack of it), an abundant assortment of arousing stimuli become available, without any of the negative side-effects of ambivalence.

All over. Most men focus their attention almost exclusively on their genitals when they masturbate. Some of these men carry the same genital focus into their partner sex. But many more are far more sensual with partners than they ever consider being with themselves. Although the genitals always retain a special erotic significance for the vast majority of people, any part of the body can respond pleasurably to touch. However, sensitivity withers away from areas which are ignored; they become less and less responsive.

Sensitivity can be revived by stimulating many different areas of the body during masturbation. One hand might be used for genital stimulation while the other hand is allowed to roam over the rest of the body, lingering at areas which capture one's attention; or both hands can be used for overall body exploration. A good way to discover the sensual or erotic potential of the entire body is to give oneself a complete massage, using a massage oil (see Freddie's pictures, pages 82 & 83). Safflower, peanut, and coconut oils are all excellent and far less expensive than commercially-packaged massage oils.

Sights. Visual self-exploration can also be pleasurable, especially for those who are responsive to visual stimulation. Some people enjoy opening their eyes at times during masturbation in order to watch their bodies change as they become aroused. Others prefer the greater visibility which a mirror provides. If, however, mirrors are used as instruments of self-criticism, they will inhibit pleasure. Unfortunately, the use of mirrors during masturbation may also increase the fear of "narcissism," discussed earlier. Once this fear subsides, however, many people find that mirrors greatly add to acceptance and appreciation of the whole body.

Diffusion. Sometimes, when attention which is usually focused on the genitals is allowed to "wander" all over the body, the person experiences a loss of intensity; sexual energy is diffused. In virtually every instance, however, any feelings of lost intensity are replaced by feelings of more expansive sensuality and eroticism. This is especially true when one discovers that sexual attention can be refocused on the genitals at any time. Focused eroticism and diffused, nurturing sensuality can be complimentary (see John's statement, page 33).

Fluctuations. Traditional expectations about sexual response—alone or with partners—call for a steadily increasing level of arousal culminating in orgasm. Only relatively quick, highly-focused sexual experiences conform to this model. Flexibility and spontaneity in sex are much more compatible with a process-oriented (rather than goal-oriented) view of sexual response. When we take our time, include the whole body, allow both focused and diffused sensations, and perhaps enjoy a variety of mental pictures along the way, flucuations in arousal are natural and inevitable.

When a man is enjoying the process of sexual response, and not simply aiming toward a goal, erections may come and go. These erection changes may be slight or dramatic. Some men find erection flucuations disconcerting or distressing.

Noticing a partial or total erection loss, he may feel compelled to *do* something—search for a better fantasy, re-focus stimulation on the penis or struggle in some other way to maintain a constant erection. Doing so diverts his attention from pleasure and play which, in turn, may bring his naturally-fluctuating response to a complete standstill.

Some people find it useful deliberately to take breaks during autoerotic sessions, allowing arousal to subside (see James' statement, page 71). Also worth trying is to masturbate without having an orgasm at all, eliminating the temptation to become goal-oriented. Slowing down and speeding up or starting and stopping, in short, "teasing" oneself can also enhance masturbation. Continuing to pleasure oneself after ejaculation is another way to shift one's focus away from orgasm. The common assumption that sexual arousal is over after ejaculation may turn out to be inaccurate. Sometimes, continued self-touching triggers another wave of excitement—and maybe another orgasm. But this is certainly not necessary for further pleasure.

Emotions. The post-orgasmic period is usually one of emotional openness. Since men are taught to mistrust and suppress emotion, the first inclination is often to escape by immediately going to sleep or doing something else. This reaction may be even more pronounced after ejaculation with a partner, especially for the man who views expressions of emotion as weak or unmasculine. Allowing feelings to surface during masturbation is conducive to fuller enjoyment of self-sexuality—and all sexual activities.

Sounds. Emerging emotions, deep breathing and intense sensations during masturbation often result in an urge to make sounds. Spontaneous vocalizations range from quiet moans or sighs, to loud groans, cries, and/or actual words. Many people, however, suppress this urge, fearing that noises will be heard by other household members or neighbors. In addition, some men erroneously believe that only women (or effeminate men) vocalize during sex. Since sounds are suppressed by tensing throat muscles and restricting breathing, pleasurable sensations may be inhibited simultan-eously. Allowing vocalizations to come and go freely can relieve the tension, and the sounds themselves may become erotic stimuli (see Lim's statement, page 51).

Conversation. Self-sexuality can be greatly enhanced by talking about it with a friend or lover. Such discussions can be fun, generate new ideas for autoerotic pleasure and, most importantly, provide some of the mutual support necessary to overcome a lifetime of anti-masturbation learning. Talking about self-sexuality with a lover has the added benefit of giving both partners detailed information about each other's preferences. Initiating conversations about self-sexuality is probably most easily done as part of a broader discussion of sexuality. The value of talking about masturbation can be undercut, however, by nervous joking (it's better to acknowledge initial nervousness openly) or by the feeling that one is confessing to or apologizing for the enjoyment of masturbation.

Partners. Although many people find it incomprehensible or uninteresting, including self-sexuality with a partner is often found exciting by those with the courage or curiosity to try it. It is the most effective means of showing one's partner exactly the type of stimulation which arouses him. It also helps both partners to see themselves as individuals, each of whom is sexually self-sufficient. And almost everyone is surprised to discover how erotic this can be, whether it is done by one or both of the partners.

An expanded version of this material, integrated with a discussion of women's self-sexuality, will be available from Down There Press late in 1981. This book will contain no sexually explicit photographs. It will be particularly useful in educational, therapeutic and other settings where explicit photographs may be considered inappropriate or too anxiety-provoking. Please write for additional information.

RECOMMENDED READINGS

Bernie Zilbergeld. **Male Sexuality**. Bantam, 1978.
> *The most articulate presentation of a non-performance-oriented model of male sexuality to date. Includes specific exercises which men can do (alone or with a partner) to enhance their sexual experiences or to help with sexual problems.*

Marc Feigen Fasteau. **The Male Machine**. Delta, 1975.
> *An unusually honest and enlightening discussion of the pressures exerted on men by masculine images and ideals. Especially useful for men who feel the limits of their traditional role.*

Joani Blank. **The Playbook For Men About Sex**. Down There Press, 1976.
> *Sexual self-awareness workbook (more play than work) for men of all ages and sexual persuasions.*

Jack Morin. **Anal Pleasure and Health**. Down There Press, available early in 1981.
> *Detailed information and step-by-step suggestions for men and women who wish to become more aware of the anal area, learn how to relax anal muscles and enjoy anal stimulation safely and comfortably, alone or with a partner.*

Betty Dodson. **Liberating Masturbation: a Meditation on Self Love**. Bodysex Designs, 1974.
> *A passionate celebration of women's self-sexuality from a feminist point of view. Contains concepts and suggestions useful to both men and women.*

POSTER

An 18" x 24", high-quality poster, based on the cover of this book, is available from Down There Press for $4.50 postpaid. Send your name, address and zip with a check made payable to:

Down There Press
P.O. Box 2086
Burlingame, CA 94010

ABOUT DOWN THERE PRESS

Down There Press was started by Joani Blank in 1975 to publish her *Playbook for Women about Sex. Men Loving Themselves* is the press' eighth title. Four new titles are planned for 1981-2. Down There Press is the only independent publisher specializing in sex education and sexual self-awareness books for adults and children.

ALSO FROM DOWN THERE PRESS

Joani Blank. **The Playbook For Women About Sex.** 1975.

Joani Blank. **Good Vibrations; The Complete Guide to Vibrators.** 1976.
> *Informal guide to the acquisition and enjoyment of vibrators for solo and partner sex play.*

Joani Blank and Honey Lee Cottrell. **I Am My Lover.** 1978.
> *The first photographic book on masturbation for women.*

Patricia Waters. **The Sensuous Coloring Book.** 1980.
> *An unusual and sophisticated coloring book for adults for use with any coloring medium.*

Joani Blank, illustrations by Marcia Quakenbush. **The Playbook For Kids About Sex.** 1980.

Jack Morin has been a photographer since he was ten. His primary work, however, is in the fields of psychology, psychotherapy and sexology. He received his Ph.D. from the Humanistic Psychology Institute, San Francisco, where his research focused on the development and testing of new sex counseling techniques. His forthcoming book, *Anal Pleasure and Health,* is based on that research. In addition to his private therapy practice, he teaches Human Sexuality at Skyline College and regularly leads workshops and seminars on male sexuality, sex counseling, intimate relationships and many other subjects.